D1599934

IRONY AND THE DISCOURSE OF MODERNITY

Irony and the Discourse of Modernity

ERNST BEHLER

UNIVERSITY OF WASHINGTON PRESS
Seattle and London

Printed in the United States of America

Library of Congress Cataloging-in-Publication Data

Behler, Ernst, 1928–
Irony and the discourse of modernity / Ernst Behler.
p. cm.
ISBN 0–295–96998–9 (alk. paper)
1. Irony in literature. 2. Modernism (Literature)
3. Postmodernism (Literature) I. Title.
PN56. I65B44 1990 90-11960
809′ .918—dc20 CIP

The paper used in this publication meets the minimum requirements of American National Standard for Information Sciences—Permanence of Paper for Printed Library Materials, ANSI Z39.48–1984. ♾

Contents

Preface

This text was originally presented as the annual faculty lecture at the University of Washington in November 1986 and, upon invitation from the University of Washington Press, expanded to its present format. In spite of considerable additions to the lecture, however, the original line of thought and argumentation has been maintained. These additions are all of an illustrative, exemplifying nature and seek to develop particular points more fully than was possible within the limited scope of the lecture.

As is customary in the faculty lectures at the University of Washington, topics of one's own research serve as the occasion for formulating issues of a broader interest. In this particular case, I tried to explore the question of our own position in history, the status of our modernity, and our relation to the tradition, through that figure of speech and writing which has received the name of irony. Irony, of course, is not to be taken in any restricted literary meaning, but in that broad mode of saying it otherwise, of circumlocution, configuration, and indirect communication characteristic of today's humanistic and scientific discourses. This investigation quite naturally led to the names and themes discussed in this text, all of which I would like to link more closely with our contemporary concerns.

Whenever they were available I have used English translations for quotations from foreign sources, but have always checked the text against the original. When no appropriate translation was available, I have provided one myself.

ERNST BEHLER
Seattle, March 1989

Abbreviations

The following abbreviations are used in the text.

AMT — Charles de Saint-Evremond, *On Ancient and Modern Tragedy,* in *The Works of M. de Saint-Evremond* (London, 1928), available in Scott Elledge and Donald Schier, eds., *The Continental Model* (Ithaca: Cornell University Press, 1970), 123–30.

AWS — August Wilhelm Schlegel, *Kritische Ausgabe seiner Vorlesungen,* ed. Ernst Behler with the collaboration of Frank Jolles, 6 vols. (Paderborn-München: Schöningh, 1989–).

BP — Blaise Pascal, *Oeuvres complètes* (Paris: Gallimard, 1956).

CI — Søren Kierkegaard, *The Concept of Irony with Constant Reference to Socrates,* trans. Lee M. Capel (New York: Harper and Row, 1965).

CIS — Richard Rorty, *Contingency, Irony, and Solidarity* (Cambridge: Cambridge University Press, 1989).

CRF — Madame de Staël, *Considérations sur la Révolution française,* ed. Jacques Godechot (Paris: Tallendier, 1983).

D — Jacques Derrida, "Différance," in *Speech and Phenomena and Other Essays on Husserl's Theory of Signs,* trans. David B. Allison and Newton Garver (Evanston: Northwestern University Press, 1973), 129–60.

DAM — Bernard le Bouvier de Fontenelle, *A Digression on the Ancients and the Moderns,* in *The Continental Model,* ed. Scott Elledge and Donald Schier (Ithaca: Cornell University Press, 1970), 358–70.

DM — Jürgen Habermas, *The Philosophical Discourse of Modernity: Twelve Lectures,* trans. Frederick Lawrence (Cambridge: MIT Press, 1987).

DP — John Dryden, "An Essay of Dramatic Poetry," in *Essays of John Dryden,* ed. W. P. Ker (New York: Russell and Russell, 1961), vol. 1, 64–126.

E — *Encyclopédie ou dictionnaire raisonné des Sciences, des Arts et des Métiers, par une Société de Gens de Lettres,* 35 vols. and 3 vols. (Geneva: Pellet, 1777).

EM — Jacques Derrida, "The Ends of Man," in *Margins of Philosophy,* trans. Alan Bass (Chicago: The University of Chicago Press, 1982), 109–36.

FN — Friedrich Nietzsche, *Kritische Studienausgabe,* ed. Giorgio Colli and Mazzino Montinari, 15 vols. (Berlin: de Gruyter, 1980).

When possible, the following Nietzsche translations were used:

- *BT* — Friedrich Nietzsche, *The Birth of Tragedy and the Case of Wagner,* trans. Walter Kaufmann (New York: Random House, 1967).
- *DB* — Friedrich Nietzsche, *Daybreak,* trans. R. J. Hollingdale (Cambridge: Cambridge University Press, 1982).

GE	Friedrich Nietzsche, *Beyond Good and Evil,* trans. Walter Kaufmann (New York: Random House, 1966).
GM	Friedrich Nietzsche, *On the Genealogy of Morals: Ecce Homo,* trans. Walter Kaufmann and R. J. Hollingdale (New York: Random House, 1969).
GS	Friedrich Nietzsche, *The Gay Science,* trans. Walter Kaufmann (New York: Random House, 1974).
HH	Friedrich Nietzsche, *Human, All Too Human. A Book for Free Spirits,* trans. R. J. Hollingdale (Cambridge: Cambridge University Press, 1986).
TI	Friedrich Nietzsche, *Twilight of the Idols: The Anti-Christ,* trans. R. J. Hollingdale (New York: Penguin Books, 1968).
UM	Friedrich Nietzsche, *Untimely Meditations,* trans. R. J. Hollingdale (Cambridge: Cambridge University Press, 1986).

FS Friedrich Schlegel, *Kritische Ausgabe seiner Werke,* ed. Ernst Behler with the collaboration of Jean-Jacques Anstett, Hans Eichner, and other specialists, 35 vols. (Paderborn-München: Schöningh, 1958–).

Translations were taken, when available, from the following edition:

LF	Friedrich Schlegel, *Lucinde and the Fragments,* trans. Peter Firchow (Minneapolis: University of Minnesota Press, 1971).

GWFH Georg Wilhelm Friedrich Hegel, *Werke in 20 Bänden* (Frankfurt: Suhrkamp Taschenbuch Wissenschaft, 1986).

HL Richard Rorty, "Habermas and Lyotard on Postmodernity," *Praxis International* 4 (1984): 32–44.

HN Martin Heidegger, *Nietzsche,* trans. David Farrell Krell and others, 4 vols. (San Francisco: Harper and Row, 1979–85).

M Jürgen Habermas, "Modernity—An Incomplete Project," trans. Seyla Ben-Habib, in Hal Foster, ed., *The Anti-Aesthetic: Essays on Postmodern Culture* (Port Townsend: Bay Press, 1983), 3–15.

OG Jacques Derrida, *Of Grammatology,* trans. Gayatri Chakravorty Spivak (Baltimore: The Johns Hopkins University Press, 1974).

OL Madame de Staël, *De la littérature considérée dans ses rapports avec les institutions sociales,* ed. Paul van Tieghem (Geneva and Paris: Droz, 1959).

PAM Charles Perrault, *Parallèle des Anciens et des Modernes en ce qui regarde les arts et les sciences,* ed. Hans Robert Jauβ (Munich: Kindler, 1964).

PC Jean-François Lyotard, *The Postmodern Condition: A Report on Knowledge,* trans. Geoff Bennington and Brian Massumi, foreword by Fredric Jameson (Minneapolis: University of Minnesota Press, 1979).

QC Jürgen Habermas, "Questions and Counterquestions," in Richard J. Bernstein, ed., *Habermas and Modernity* (Cambridge: MIT Press, 1986), 192–216.

R David Hume, *Of the Rise and the Progress of the Arts and the Sciences,* in *Essays, Literary, Moral and Political* (London: Ward, Lock, and Co., n.d.), 63–79.

SSP Jacques Derrida, "Structure, Sign, and Play in the Discourse of the Human Sciences," in *Writing and Difference,* trans. Alan Bass (Chicago: The University of Chicago Press, 1978), 278–93.

SW Heinrich Heine, *Sämtliche Werke*, ed. Klaus Briegleb (Munich: Hanser, 1971).

TA Jacques Derrida, *D'un ton apocalyptique adopté naguère en philosophie* (Paris: Editions Galilée, 1983).

IRONY AND THE DISCOURSE OF MODERNITY

1
Modernism and Postmodernism in Contemporary Thought

Among the dominant themes in today's critical and philosophical debate, the question of what constitutes the particular status of our modernity seems to gain in scope and interest almost every day. The literature on the designation of various modernities, the roots of our own modernity, epochal breaks, or change of paradigms in our mode of knowledge is constantly growing. All this reflects, of course, our own historical position at the end of the twentieth century. The quest, however, for what is modern and the search for the specific features of modernism are as old as the modern age itself as it originated with Bacon and Descartes. A self-reflective consciousness of time combined with a need for self-assurance accompany the modern age through all its phases, and this quite naturally. For being modern means essentially a departure from exemplary models of the past, a decentering of habitual ways of viewing the world, and the necessity for producing normative standards out of oneself. This is combined with an opening to the future which has the necessary result that the moment of a new beginning constituting modernity will incessantly produce itself again and again.

These considerations have come forth since the late seventeenth century in a certain type of semiphilosophical, semiliterary writing that thematizes the topic of modernity and simultaneously exhibits its problematic nature. For writing about modernity, especially one's own, is an act that inevitably engenders history and relegates modernity to the past. No direct way of writing can escape from this paradox. As the most extreme expression of time, modernity is like an endless fuse cord that keeps consuming itself. Regarding this inherent paradox, Nietzsche wrote, "Being is only an uninterrupted has-been, a thing that lives by negating, consuming and contradicting itself."[1] With only a seemingly different twist of thought, Foucault declared it to be the task of philosophy to explain today and that which we are today. Yet he also recommended doing this without declaring today as the moment of the greatest damnation or the daybreak of the dawning sun and added, "No, it is a day like every other day or rather a day never precisely like the others."[2]

I

It is from these considerations that the notion of the postmodern, of postmodernity, has originated—a notion that because of its enhanced paradoxical structure has become a real annoyance to some of my colleagues in the humanities. The prefix *post* seems to suggest—as in postcapitalist, poststructuralist, postfeminist, or postnuclear—a new period, another epoch after a former one, a relief, so to speak, from the past, and, because of a lack of a new designation, contents itself with canceling out the previous system without completely deleting it. Yet in the case of postmodern, this does not work, because modern is already the most advanced period designation and cannot be outdone. Postmodernity therefore reveals itself as an ironic notion communicating indirectly, by way of circumlocution, configuration, and bafflement, the

1. Friedrich Nietzsche, "On the Uses and Disadvantages of History for Life," in *Friedrich Nietzsche, Untimely Meditations*, trans. R.J. Hollingdale (Cambridge: Cambridge University Press, 1983), 61.

2. Michel Foucault, "Um welchen Preis sagt die Vernunft die Wahrheit?—Ein Gespräch," *Spuren-Zeitschrift für Kunst und Gesellschaft* nos. 1–2 (1983):7.

necessity and impossibility of discussing the status of modernity in a straightforward and meaningful manner. Postmodernity, in its twisted posture, seems to be the awareness of this paradox, and consequently of the status of modernity, in a somersaulting fashion.

This seems to be at least the most general connotation of the term in many of today's writings. From here, postmodernity appears to be that attitude in which the problems, questions, and issues of modernity accumulate in an unheard-of way, which explains the constant references to forerunners, to anticipations of postmodernism in previous centuries, to writers such as Nietzsche or Diderot. Postmodernism is neither an overcoming of modernity nor a new epoch, but a critical continuation of modernism which is itself both critique and criticism. Criticism now turns against itself, and postmodernism thereby becomes a radicalized, intensified version of modernism, as would seem to be implied through a certain nuance in the prefix *post*. A comparison of postmodernism to the notion of avant-garde seems to confirm this impression, because avant-garde clearly gives us the idea of outdoing, of advancing, of a future-oriented innovation, whereas the retrospective attitude of postmodernism seems to relate to the past, if only through self-criticism and self-doubt.

Yet with equal reason, we can see postmodernism as that situation in which all the ideals of modernity have come to their exhaustion, that phase which claims to have experienced the end of metaphysics, the end of philosophy, and the end of man. We should be careful, however, not to construe these events as the beginning of a new period, as unavoidable as it may seem for us to think in such categories. For if postmodernism opened an entirely new phase of intellectual history, of antimodernism or the accomplished transgression of modernism, it would continue the innovative trend of modernity, something which seems to be precluded by the paradoxical configuration of its name. One good way of expressing this feature would be to say that the postmodernist mind is just as skeptical about the historical designation of epochs as it is about structural unification in terms of system.

From this latter perspective, postmodernism is the rejection of any totalized conception of truth in the sense of global philosophies of history, all-embracing systems of meaning, or uniform foundations of knowledge. What motivates the post-modern mentality instead can be described as a radical pluralism of thought and opinion, without the presumption, however, that such a state of plurality and openness will ever be fully realized. What is certain in the given situation is heterogeneity in discourse and fallibility in theory formation. Historically speaking, postmodernism is an alignment with Nietzsche's perspectivism and the refusal of Hegelianism, of Hegel's equation of truth with totality, as well as of his entire teleology. Another way of describing postmodernism would be through semiotics, by saying that in our society the relationship between signifier and signified is no longer intact, in that signs do not refer to something signified, a pregiven entity, but always to other signs. We thus never reach the true meaning of things, but only other signs, interpretations of other signs, interpretations of interpretations, and we move along in an endless chain of signification.

We could try to say that postmodernism protects the position of the other side, that of the nonsystem, of the woman, the suppressed minority, although we would soon discover that any accusatory criticism combined with rectifying tendencies in the style of ideology critique or even in the old tradition of liberalism would run counter to the antisystematic and atotalitarian drive in postmodernist thinking. Such a critique would eventually be seen as a sign of the reemerging system and of superimposed value structures. It would similarly be questionable to claim that the tradition of modern thought from Kierkegaard to Sartre, existentialism in other words, already articulated the groundlessness and finitude which became decisive in postmodernism. This would be a false canon because groundlessness and infinitude are experienced in existentialism as a deficiency, whereas in postmodernism this experience is one of "joyful wisdom," of "gaya scienzia." Postmodernism affirms the "anything goes that works" device in a cheerful mood of self-deprecation and parody. Writing is the main activity of postmodernism. But to write on postmodernism in the form of a handbook or an encyclopedic article would be self-deception.

It would of course be fatuous to restrict the postmodernist mood to theory and philosophy without recognizing similar trends in other areas of life. Architecture is, if not the origin of this movement, then one of its most conspicuous expressions. Fredric Jameson has shown that contemporary architectural trends in the arrangement of our cities or individual buildings counteract fundamental concerns of the modern and rationalist mentality. In their tendency toward the mere surface, the epidermis, the skin, and by eliminating any "depth dimension" (for instance, in Los Angeles), these architectural trends offset traditional models of building characteristic of the modern phase, such as the dialectical model of essence and appearance, the psychoanalytical model of latent and manifest, the existentialist model of authenticity and nonauthenticity, the Marxist model of alienation and reconciliation, and the semiotic model of signifier and signified.[3]

3. Fredric Jameson, "Postmodernism, or the Cultural Logic of Late Capitalism," *New Left Review* 146 (July/August 1984): 53–92. See also Hal Foster, ed., *The Anti-Aesthetic: Essays on Postmodern Culture* (Port Townsend: Bay Press,

In the more general sphere of aesthetic life and aesthetic production, these trends find their correspondence in an extension of art to mass society and mass culture. In a now famous image, Adorno once illustrated the modern notion of an elitist autonomy of art with Odysseus's voyage through the realm of the Sirens.[4] Tied to the mast of his boat, he could listen to the seductive singing of the nymphs without succumbing to their attempt to lure him into death, while his deafened sailors oared him through the dangerous zone. This is at least one aspect of this image. In the postmodern relationship to art, the separation of classes is supposedly overcome. The price for this accomplishment, however, is a leveling of art to the standards of a mass culture, an absorption of art by the vulgarity of life. Art is no longer the realm of otherness, no longer able to hold a mirror, to point a finger. One especially striking example of this development is the museum and the hedonistic use of the museum in postmodernist practice. Originally an institution, a temple for the preservation and exhibition of art objects that otherwise would not have survived, the museum has become a postmodernist architectural building surrounded by shops and restaurants where objects of exhibition are evaluated according to economic standards. Computerized data inform about the showability of the museum's possessions and regulate their acquisition and sale.[5] Conversely, and again in accordance with the anything-goes device, purpose-oriented

1983); and Heinrich Klotz, ed., *Postmodern Visions: Drawings, Paintings, and Models by Contemporary Architects* (New York: Abbeville Press, 1985).

4. Max Horkheimer and Theodor W. Adorno, *Dialectic of Enlightenment*, trans. John Cumming (New York: Herder and Herder, 1972), 32–34.

5. Christa Bürger, "Das Verschwinden der Kunst: Die Postmoderne-Debatte in den USA," in *Postmoderne: Alltag, Allegorie und Avantgarde*, ed. Christa and Peter Bürger (Frankfurt: Suhrkamp, 1987), 48–49.

activities based entirely on profit, such as advertising, assume the lofty *l'art pour l'art* attitude of complete purposelessness. This populist image of postmodernism is interwoven with complex theoretical and philosophical issues. They have come forth in a body of texts marked by an intensified critique of reason and rationality, a bewildering questioning of those values and norms which have governed the course of modern history.

Yet it remains doubtful whether postmodernism has one particular style of expression or one particular area where the postmodern attitude can be seen in its true identity. Non-identity, oscillating otherness, seems to be the postmodern mode of expression, and the realm of existence for the post-modern mode is precisely there where it presently is not. For philosophers, the postmodern style appears to be more strictly given in literature and critical theory than in philosophy, for literary critics more in architecture, for specialists in architecture perhaps in advertising, and so on. Prototypes of postmodernism are hard to locate and always outdone by something else. Poststructuralism is outdone by deconstruction and deconstruction by what is called the new historicism. For writers in the postmodern style, the evasiveness of their subject matter goes hand in hand with a certain superficiality or even dilettantism in their expertise, a certain "poor philology," a transgression of limits. Postmodern lectures are taped, postmodern texts are photocopied, and postmodern writings are put onto the word processor.

2

Jean-François Lyotard's *The Postmodern Condition: A Report on Knowledge* of 1979 is the theoretical text most directly concerned with these issues.[6] As is obvious from its title, the writing is not meant to be an event in itself or an original moment in the evolution of postmodernism, but poses as a comment on a pregiven situation, as a report to the Council of Universities of the government of Quebec on a research project devoted to the "condition of knowledge in the most highly developed societies." The text is a summary of what has happened in the past decade under the headings of post-structuralism, deconstruction, and critique of metaphysics. Yet Lyotard also coins the terms and concepts which have guided or challenged the discussion of these events ever since. The most prominent among them is the term postmodern itself, occurring right at the beginning: "Our working hypothesis is that the status of knowledge is altered as societies enter what is known as the postindustrial age and cultures enter what is known as the postmodern age" (*PC*, 3). By using, however, the paradoxical notion of postmodern with the casual connotation of postindustrial, and by introducing in the context of a report the contemporary crisis of knowledge as a "crisis of narratives," the text is a full-blown postmodern phenomenon itself, with all the ironic postures and configurations required for this style.

Lyotard's characterization of postmodernism has various aspects, the most direct of which is perhaps the idea of a transformation of knowledge, even a "mercantilization of knowledge" (*PC*, 26). The issue is that of a fundamental change in the conception of knowledge that has essentially affected its nature. The criterion of knowledge in the post-

6. Jean-François Lyotard, *The Postmodern Condition: A Report on Knowledge*, trans. Geoff Bennington and Brian Massumi, foreword by Fredric Jameson (Minneapolis: University of Minnesota Press, 1979). References to this text are designated *PC*.

modern phase is translatability into computer language, into quantities of information (*PC*, 23), whereby the old ideal of knowledge as a formation of the mind and the personality dies out and is replaced by a conception of knowledge in terms of suppliers and users, of commodity producers and consumers (*PC*, 24). Knowledge becomes a major stake in the worldwide competition for power (*PC*, 26). Another way of describing this state of knowledge would be to say that postmodernism is the departure from any totalizing attempt of reasoning, from any ultimate foundation of truth.

The most famous formulation of this diagnosis is Lyotard's remark that in postmodernism one no longer believes in "metanarratives." Metanarratives are those comprehensive as well as foundational discourses in which all details of knowledge and human activity find ultimate sense and meaning. Examples of such metadiscourses or metanarratives are the grand antique, medieval, or rational philosophies, Platonism, for instance, or the great religions of humanity, the utopias of a final unity, reconciliation, and harmony. Lyotard distinguishes between metanarratives of a mythological and of a rational nature and even attributes different periods in the history of humanity to them. In the premodern world, one justified one's culture through narrations of a mythological or religious character and founded all institutions, social and political practices, laws, ethics, and manners of thinking on a belief in these metanarratives. The modern period began when these founding narratives were no longer mythical or religious, but became rational and philosophical, and secured a meaningful procedure not through a god or a heroic lawgiver, but through the authority of reason. Although rational in their manner of argumentation, they were still narratives because they gave meaning through a projected odyssey with a redemptive type of foundation such as the acquisition of freedom, progressive emancipation, the all-round human personality, or accomplished socialism and welfare. All human realities found a firm basis in these ideas. Good examples of these metanarratives of a rational and modern order are for Lyotard the dialectics of spirit, the emancipation of the rational or the working subject, the hermeneutics of meaning, or the creation of wealth through capitalist techno-science. In a certain way, Hegel's dialectics of spirit contains all these narratives and can therefore be considered the quintessence of speculative modernity.

Postmodernism, in a word then, is incredulity in the face of such universal metanarratives. They have not been refuted but simply become outworn; they no longer fulfill their function of bestowing sense and meaning upon human activities. They also no longer serve as a foundation for the discourse of the individual sciences, which instead follow their own rules and break up the one grand metadiscourse into myriads of individual languages, of language games and language rules in the respective scientific contexts. Lyotard likes to condense this feature by using Habermas's notion of a "crisis of legitimation," of a crumbling legitimacy of authority, but he expands the notion far beyond any state, government, or institutionalized power to a generalized fading away of all overriding authority and legitimacy. For what the classical metanarratives did can very well be characterized as a legitimizing of all particular forms of knowledge, of all individual scientific discourses, those of justice as well as those of truth (*PC*, 33). After these metadiscourses have been dismissed by incredulity, the question of the legitimacy of knowledge comes up again in a different manner (*PC*, 112) and certainly cannot be resolved by another form of totalization, by the invention of a new metadiscourse (*PC*, 109).

Lyotard considers individual language systems as they exist

in the individual sciences to be the type of relationship necessary for the existence of society (*PC*, 56) and, in reference to Wittgenstein, likes to call these discourses language games. He thereby emphasizes the pragmatic aspect in their different ways of enunciation and their inherent rules, but also, what is perhaps more important, the "agonistic" character in and among these games (*PC*, 41). Rules have no legitimacy in themselves and rest on agreement, on consensus among the players. Yet, as in a game of chess, each new move creates a new situation (*PC*, 40).

We should be careful, however, not to construe Lyotard's report on knowledge in the postmodern stage and his thesis of a breakup of one great metanarrative into a multiplicity of individual language games as the new metadiscourse of the postmodern period. He expressly denies any originality or truth value for his account and considers it to be of hypothetical character at best, of strategic value with regard to the point in question, that is, capable of emphasizing certain aspects (*PC*, 31). Similarly, we should not think about these periods of premodern, modern, and postmodern as having datable ruptures or definite epochal breaks, because their contents and styles overlap in terms of time. The premodern type of mythical and religious legitimation can linger on into the postmodern period just as postmodern scepticism can be found among writers of the premodern age. The premodern, modern, and postmodern modes of legitimation and delegitimation depicted by Lyotard are perhaps best viewed as ideal types. They have, however, also a clearly historical connotation, in that they dominate periods of history. Of special interest in this regard is the relationship between the modern and the postmodern styles. Lyotard maintains that the postmodern manner of thinking does not situate itself after or against the modern, but is enclosed in it, although in hidden fashion. To think about history in a straightforward line is entirely modern, as demonstrated by Christianity, Cartesianism, and Jacobinism. The disappearance of the term "avant-garde" with its military flavor is an indication of the withering away of modernity, because this term is an expression of that old-fashioned modernity at which we are now able to smile.[7]

In a speech of 1980 with the programmatic title "Modernity—An Incomplete Project,"[8] which is now already historical but has had several follow-ups in subsequent writings, Jürgen Habermas attempted to rescue modernity from its postmodernist detractors. He clearly took postmodernity as antimodernity, as an attempt that sacrifices "the tradition of modernity in order to make room for a new historicism" (*M*, 3), an "anarchistic intention of blowing up the continuum of history," and a "rebelling against all that is normative" (*M*, 5). Although this text focused on the "aesthetic modernity" of dadaists and surrealists in the "Café Voltaire" (*M*, 5), Habermas also ventured into the broader aspects of modernism as based on three autonomous spheres of reason (science, morality, and art), three realms with an "inner logic" and a validity of their own: cognitive-instrumental, moral-practical, and aesthetic-expressive rationality (*M*, 9). Whereas enlightened philosophers of the late eighteenth century distinguished these different types of legitimizing reason for the enrichment of life, the twentieth century has shattered this optimism by abandoning the autonomy of these segments to

7. Some of these ideas are taken up and further developed in Jean-François Lyotard, *Le postmoderne expliqué aux enfants* (Paris: Les Editions de Minuit, 1986).

8. Jürgen Habermas, "Modernity—An Incomplete Project," trans. Seyla Ben-Habib, in Foster, *The Anti-Aesthetic*, 3–15. References to this text are designated *M*. For further discussions of the topic see Richard J. Bernstein, ed., *Habermas and Modernity* (Cambridge: MIT Press, 1986).

specialists and thereby separating them from everyday communication.

This is for Habermas the crisis of modernity in its most global aspect. His attitude toward this basic problem, however, is obvious from his rhetorical question, "should we try to hold on to the *intentions* of the Enlightenment, feeble as they may be, or should we declare the entire project of modernity a lost cause?" (*M*, 9). The answer is of course a rejection of the postmodernists' "false negation of culture" (*M*, 11) and a maintenance of "communicative rationality," of "reproduction and transmission of values and norms" (*M*, 8) in Habermas's sense. More directly, he says: "I think that instead of giving up modernity and its project as a lost cause, we should learn from the mistakes of those extravagant programs which have tried to negate modernity" (*M*, 12). In a rhetorical move hard to comprehend, however, Habermas labels all postmodern critics of the modern type of rationality as "neoconservatives" (*M*, 6–7), and with a revealing myopia characterizes the French critics, all of his own generation if not considerably older, as "young conservatives," and describes them as a line that "leads from Georges Bataille via Michel Foucault to Jacques Derrida." They claim, according to Habermas, "revelations of a decentered subjectivity emancipated from the imperatives of work and usefulness, and with this experience they step outside the modern world" (*M*, 14). As Habermas sees it, these writers juxtapose with instrumental reason "a principle only accessible through evocation, be it the will to power or sovereignity, Being or the Dionysiac force of the poetical" (*M*, 14).

This image of irrationalism is of course just as questionable as the equation of postmodernism with conservatism. On the contrary, it is Habermas's critique of postmodernism and its foundationalist drive that shows a spontaneous alliance with a traditionalist, conservative fundamentalism of basic values and basic norms. Lyotard's response to Habermas, therefore, is entitled *Postmodernism for Children* and presents itself as a collection of letters put together by editors who want to protect the author against the "reproach of irrationalism, neoconservatism, intellectual terrorism, simple-minded liberalism, nihilism, and cynism."[9] On the whole, the letters suggest that we seem to have entered a "phase of slackening." Many symptoms indicate this, as for instance, the writings of a thinker of repute (that is, Habermas) who wants to defend the uncompleted project of modernity against neoconservatives by opening the way to a unity of experience. In his later writings, especially in *The Differend,*[10] Lyotard moves away from any attempt to construe postmodernism as a completely new manner of life and thought and eliminates any traces of a progressive, revolutionary, utopian, or anarchistic, that is, modern conception of postmodernism that his earlier writings might still bear.[11]

3

The main thing Habermas did in response to the postmodern critique of reason and rationality was to construe a new metanarrative of emancipatory reason which attempts to set things right and also to assign the French critics their proper

9. Lyotard, *Le postmoderne expliqué aux enfants,* 3. The first section, "Answering the Question: What Is Postmodernism?" is included in English translation in Lyotard, *The Postmodern Condition,* 71–82.

10. Jean-François Lyotard, *Le différend* (Paris: Les Editions de Minuit, 1983). See also his "Grundlagenkrise," *Neue Hefte für Philosophie* 26 (1986): 1–33.

11. See especially Jean-François Lyotard, *Dérive à partir de Marx et Freud* (Paris: Union générale des éditions, 1973), and the concept of "désirévolution" in that text.

position. He admits that it was mainly the challenge from the other side of the Rhine that motivated him to reconstruct the "philosophical discourse of modernity" in a book of the same title.[12] In this new metanarrative, Habermas mobilizes the entirety of modern philosophy from a Germano-centered perspective. The heroes of this epic are Kant, Hegel, Marx, and Habermas. Their detractors form the "line" from the romantics to Nietzsche, Mallarmé, Dadaists, Foucault, and Derrida. Horkheimer and Adorno played into their hands but distinguished themselves from totalized scepticism by adopting from Walter Benjamin an attitude called "hopeless hope." Max Weber's theme of an independent logic of value spheres such as science, morality, and art provides the structure of this tale, and its content is the relentless drive for self-assurance on the part of modernity.

The beginning in this journey of the modern spirit is Kant, who "installed reason in the supreme seat of judgment before which anything that made a claim to validity had to be justified" (*DM,* 18). Through his three critiques, Kant subdivided reason into the faculties of theoretical reason (*Critique of Pure Reason*), practical reason (*Critique of Practical Reason*), and aesthetic judgment (*Critique of Judgment*) and thereby established special courts for the three cultural spheres of philosophy and metaphysics, morality and law, and aesthetics and poetics. Such a division grounded all these three spheres in rational foundations of their own. Yet Kant did not perceive these differentiations as completely different tracks without any relationship to one another, as "diremptions." He therefore only introduced the modern spirit, which for Habermas is

12. Jürgen Habermas, *The Philosophical Discourse of Modernity: Twelve Lectures,* trans. Frederick Lawrence (Cambridge: MIT Press, 1987). References to this text are designated *DM.*

inspired by the need for a deeper foundation, an "ideal intrinsic form," that is entirely derived from the spirit of modernity and not imposed upon it from outside (*DM*, 19–20). We must therefore turn to Hegel, who in reality was the first to raise the detachment of modernity from founding and external norms to the levels of a philosophical problem (*DM*, 16). With him the need for "*self-reassurance* of modernity" comes to such a head that it becomes the "*fundamental problem* of his own philosophy" (*DM*, 16). Hegel discovered the principle of modernity as a "structure of self-relation," a full deployment of all human potentialities, and called this principle subjectivity (*DM*, 16).

In the principle of subjectivity, all autonomous spheres of the modern world appear to be gathered in a focal point. However, Hegel's concept of "absolute knowledge" remains encircled in subjectivity and no longer permits a critique of subjectivity from any external position (*DM*, 34). Hegel's notion of the absolute has the advantage of comprehending modernity in terms of its own principle (*DM*, 36), but this solution does not completely satisfy because the critique of subjectivity (modernity) can be carried out "only within the framework of the philosophy of the subject" (*DM*, 41). Such philosophizing obliterates the intrinsic tensions of modernity and does not fully meet the need for self-assurance. The unrest and movement of modernity therefore explode this concept at the moment of its conception (*DM*, 41).

Hegel's disciples freed the critique of modernity from the burden of the Hegelian concept of reason (*DM*, 53), but maintained the task of a self-assurance of modernity (*DM*, 58). Marx transformed the concept of reflection to the concept of production and replaced self-consciousness with labor (*DM*, 59). With Nietzsche and his followers, a new discourse enters the scene, no longer willing to hold on to the principle of reason in the critique of modernity, but taking critique out of the hands of reason and striking "the subjective genitive from the phrase 'critique of reason'" (*DM*, 59). From now on, whichever name philosophy assumes in this tradition—fundamental ontology (Heidegger), critique or negative dialectics (Adorno), deconstruction (Derrida), or genealogy (Foucault)—these pseudonyms for Habermas are only "the cloak for a scantily concealed end of philosophy" (*DM*, 53). With its professed "antihumanism," this tradition constitutes the "real challenge" for Habermas and his discourse of modernity. Before Habermas can investigate "what lies hidden behind the radical gestures of this challenge," however, he has to conduct a closer inspection of the type of antireason represented by his father figures, Horkheimer and Adorno.

Such an examination appears all the more important because the contemporary French interpretation of Nietzsche has brought about moods and attitudes confusingly similar to those conjured up by Horkheimer and Adorno, and Habermas would like "to forestall this confusion" (*DM*, 106). What appears to be the particular mark of these two representatives of the Frankfurt School in contrast to their French counterparts in the critique of reason is their use of Benjamin's "hope of the hopeless," or their own "now paradoxical labor of conceptualization" (*DM*, 106). To put it in different terms, they realized only too well the injuries caused by "instrumentalized" reason, the coercion of systematized conceptual thought, and the pretensions of utopian reconciliations. Yet they maintained Hegelian wholeness and integrity in the structural patterns of their thought by lamenting its absence and unrealizability as a lack, a loss, a deficiency and not, as in poststructuralist and postmodern thought, as the appropriate human condition. They suffered from this situation and increased their suffering by insisting on a critique of reason through reason, and by not giving in to a prerational, supra-rational, or transsubjective, but in any event irrational, lapse into myth as Nietzsche and his French followers have done according to Habermas.

The resistance to myth is so strong for Horkheimer and Adorno, Habermas claims, that it forms a central motif in their critique of the Enlightenment.[13] As a matter of fact, this critique can be summarized as the "thesis of a secret complicity" of myth and enlightenment, in that "myth is already enlightenment" and "enlightenment reverts to mythology" (*DM,* 107). The prime example of this "entwinement" is Homer's *Odyssey,* interpreted by Horkheimer and Adorno as the "primal history of subjectivity" (*DM,* 108), the epic anticipation of Hegel's *Phenomenology of Spirit.* This "myth of origin" depicts the double meaning of emancipation, of "springing from," namely, "a shudder at being uprooted and a sigh of relief at escaping." The "cunning of Odysseus" represents the modern mentality of buying off the curse of vengeful powers by offering vicarious victims (*DM,* 108). The song of the Sirens recalls for Odysseus a "happiness once guaranteed by the 'fluctuating interrelationship with nature,'" but he has this experience only "as one who already knows himself in chains" (*DM,* 109). Similarly, the process of enlightenment in the modern age has not resulted in liberation, but in a world upon which rests "the curse of demonic reification and deadly isolation." The permanent sign of the Enlightenment for Horkheimer and Adorno is "domination over an objectified external nature and a repressed internal nature" (*DM,* 110).

In less image-laden language we could say that for Horkheimer and Adorno, the result of the Enlightenment for the sciences is an instrumentalized type of reason solely based on

13. See Horkheimer and Adorno, *Dialectic of Enlightenment.*

technical utility; for morality and law, ethical scepticism unable to distinguish morality from immorality; and for aesthetics, mass culture that fuses art with entertainment (*DM,* 111–12). Altogether, reason is stripped of all "validity claim and assimilated to sheer power" (*DM,* 112). For Habermas, however, Horkheimer and Adorno's "critique of instrumental reason" is an amazing leveling of cultural modernity that does not do justice to what Weber had called its "stubborn differentiation of value spheres" (*DM,* 112). Habermas refers to the "specific theoretical dynamic that continually pushes the sciences," the "universalistic foundations of law and morality" in democratic will formation as well as in individual identity formation, and the "productivity and explosive power of basic aesthetic experiences" (*DM,* 113). *The Dialectic of the Enlightenment* is therefore an "odd book," the "blackest book" by Horkheimer and Adorno, and "we no longer share this mood, this attitude" (*DM,* 106). Considering the desolate emptiness of emancipation depicted by these authors, the reader, Habermas claims, correctly gets the feeling that this leveling presentation "failed to notice essential characteristics of cultural modernity" (*DM,* 114).

To illustrate Horkheimer and Adorno's extremism, Habermas concentrates on a single aspect in their critique of reason, namely, ideology critique. Since Marx, ideology critique has continued the process of the enlightenment and self-assurance of modernity by unmasking remnant mythological components in theoretical constructs supposedly free from any ensnarement in myth (*DM,* 115). Ideology critique had been especially successful in uncovering the "inadmissible mixture of power and validity" and for the first time had made enlightened reason entirely reflective, that is, a performance on its own products—theories (*DM,* 116). Ideology critique had never been entirely negative about its subject matters but was able to decipher in misused ideas "a piece of extant reason hidden from itself," or in other words, "surplus forces of productivity" (*DM*, 117–18). With Horkheimer and especially Adorno, ideology critique attained a "second-order of reflectiveness" and turned against its own foundations (*DM*, 116). Critique became total and retained nothing it could refer to as a standard. Adorno was fully aware of the "performative contradiction inherent in a totalized critique," but also convinced that we have to remain in its circle (*DM*, 119).

One option for a "critique that attacks the presuppositions of its own validity" is what Habermas considers to be Nietzsche's and Foucault's doctrine of the will to power. In its regressiveness, this option breaks out of the horizon of modernity and is bottomless as theory, because of the suspension of any distinction between power claims and truth claims (*DM*, 127). Horkheimer and Adorno's option was to shun theory and to "practice determinate negation on an *ad hoc* basis," standing firm against any fusion of reason and power in an "uninhibited scepticism" (*DM*, 128–29). Habermas's own solution, as he argued against Horkheimer and Adorno, "is to leave at least one rational criterion intact for their explanation of the corruption of all rational criteria" (*DM*, 127). This criterion is to be found in the "communicating community of researchers," in a "mediating kind of thinking," in "argumentative discourse," and is essentially "the unforced force of the better argument" (*DM*, 130). It is hard to comprehend, however, how this principle of communicative, argumentative discourse escapes the "totalized" critique of basic standards, norms, and values that Habermas deplores so vividly. By holding on to this principle of criticism and by declaring one argument "better" than the other, Habermas seems to break off critical discourse and to posit himself and his followers into the position of those who simply know better or, to borrow words from Hegel's *Phenomenology of Spirit,* into the community of those who know themselves to be the knowing ones.[14]

4

To summarize the dispute, we could say that Habermas makes a desperate effort to reaffirm the modern position of rational enlightenment and progress, whereas Lyotard has crossed the bridge to a postmodern phase in which such concerns are simply smiled at. This is basically how Richard Rorty sees the positions of the two parties. Habermas is holding on to the metanarrative of emancipation, branding scepticism of absolutes as relativism, whereas Lyotard is quite happy with relativism, historicism, and the narratives of the smaller sort, seeing no necessity to ground them in an absolute foundation. Rorty says: "To accuse postmodernism of relativism is to try to put a metanarrative in the postmodern's mouth. One will do this if one identifies 'holding a philosophical position' with having a metanarrative available. If we insist on such a definition of 'philosophy,' then postmodernism is post-philosophical. But it would be better to change the definition."[15]

Yet Rorty by no means takes his own position simply on the side of Lyotard's sceptical postmodernism. He distances himself equally from both Habermas's totalitarian foundationalism and Lyotard's elusive cynicism. Instead, he maintains a matter-of-fact pragmatism of small solutions and relative decisions which can, however, be seen as a new and interesting

14. G. W. F. Hegel, *Phenomenology of Spirit,* trans. A. V. Miller (Oxford: Oxford University Press, 1977), 409.

15. Richard Rorty, "Postmodernist Bourgeois Liberalism," *The Journal of Philosophy* 80 (1983): 589.

configuration of the postmodern stance. What he objects to in the new French narrative told by Foucault, Lyotard, and the like is not so much the naive image of science implied in these texts (*HL,* 33),[16] or a secret, hidden fascination with the German tale about the "self-assurance" of modern society (*HL,* 39), but a complete detachment from any human and social concern, the attitude of supposedly dispassionate observation, writing without a human face, the lack of formulas using "we" in these texts, and the absence of any rhetoric of emancipation in this style (*HL,* 40). This is a "remoteness" for Rorty which is reminiscent of the "conservative who pours cold water on hopes for reform, who affects to look at the problems of his fellow-citizens with the eye of the future historian" (*HL,* 41). Whereas Habermas appears to be inspired by foundationalist fervor, these French texts emanate a "dryness" which is too aloof from any type of "concrete social engineering." Rorty certainly agrees with Lyotard that "studies of the communicative competence of a transhistorical subject are of little use in reinforcing our sense of identification with our community," but he still insists on "the importance of that sense" (*HL,* 41).

With regard to Habermas's demand for "communicative competence" as the one valid standard for rational critique after all other standards have broken down, Rorty thinks that this does not really solve the problem. According to him, "there is no way for the citizens of *Brave New World* to work their way out from their happy slavery by theory," since everything they sense as rational or as "undistorted communication" will already be in accordance with their desires. Rorty says, "There is no way for us to prove to ourselves that we are

16. Richard Rorty, "Habermas and Lyotard on Postmodernity," *Praxis International* 4 (1984): 32–44. References to this text are designated *HL.*

not happy slaves of this sort, any more than to prove that our life is not a dream" (*HL,* 35). He is particularly amused by Habermas's belief in the "internal theoretical dynamic" of the sciences that supposedly propels them "beyond the creation of technologically exploitable knowledge," which he sees not so much as "theoretical dynamic" but as "social practice," something to be derived from the "social virtues of the European bourgeoisie" or simply from "theoretical curiosity." That view would take away from science the false appearance of an "ahistorical teleology" and make modern science look more like "something which a certain group of human beings invented in the same sense in which these same people can be said to have invented Protestantism, parliamentary government, and Romantic poetry" (*HL,* 36).

As to the three cultural spheres of science, morality, and art and the need for their unification in a common ground, Rorty thinks that these are artificial problems created by taking Kant and Hegel too seriously. Once one has started this division, however, the overcoming of the split will haunt one as the "fundamental philosophical problem" and result in "an endless series of reductionist and anti-reductionist moves":

> Reductionists will try to make everything scientific ("positivism"), or political (Lenin), or aesthetic (Baudelaire, Nietzsche). Anti-reductionists will show what such attempts leave out. To be a philosopher of the "modern" sort is precisely to be unwilling either to let these spheres simply co-exist uncompetitively, or to reduce the other two to the remaining one. Modern philosophy has consisted in forever realigning them, squeezing them together, and forcing them apart again. But it is not clear that these efforts have done the modern age much good (or, for that matter, harm). (*HL,* 37)

As is obvious from these observations, Rorty puts Habermas into the modern camp and attributes to himself a postmodern position. His postmodernism, however, goes beyond mere scepticism toward metanarratives and extends to practical attitudes in the art of living and thinking, such as theoretical curiosity or an "intellectual analogue of civic virtue—tolerance, irony, and a willingness to let spheres of culture flourish without worrying too much about their 'common ground,'" and so on (*HL*, 38). He thinks that Habermas "is scratching where it does not itch" (*HL*, 34), and that his story of modern philosophy is "both too pessimistic and too German" (*HL*, 38–39). Rorty would arrange the story of the modern age in a different way and construe it, for example, as "successive attempts to shake off the sort of ahistorical structure exemplified by Kant's division of culture into three 'value-spheres'" (*HL*, 39). Yet he would also refrain from telling his story the French way, in the dry manner Foucault and Lyotard are relating it, that is, completely detached from any interest in humanity and any identity with our community (*HL*, 40–41).

Rorty's type of story could just as well assume the shape of a combination of the two narratives. This story would not unmask in the German manner a "power called 'ideology' in the name of something not created by power called 'validity' or 'emancipation,'" but would simply explain in the French manner "who was currently getting and using power for what purposes." But unlike the French narrative, Rorty's story would also suggest how some other people might get power and "use it for other purposes" (*HL*, 41–42). The value of "undistorted communication" would clearly be recognized, but the need for a "theory of communicative competence as backup" could be dismissed (*HL*, 41). Another way of arranging the story for Rorty would be to minimize the importance of the "canonical sequence of philosophers from Descartes to Nietzsche" and to consider this tradition as a "distraction from the history of concrete social engineering which made the contemporary North Atlantic culture what it is now." Rorty also suggests creating "a new canon" based on an "awareness of new social and religious and institutional possibilities" instead of "developing a new dialectical twist in metaphysics and epistemology" (*HL*, 41). "That would be a way of splitting the difference between Habermas and Lyotard, of having things both ways," he says. "We could agree with Lyotard that we need no more metanarratives, but with Habermas that we need less dryness" (*HL*, 41). Yet Rorty's postmodernism comes forth best in terms of John Dewey's philosophy, in taking seriously "Dewey's suggestion that the way to re-enchant the world, to bring back what religion gave our forefathers, is to stick to the concrete" (*HL*, 42), and he concludes, "Those who want beautiful social harmonies want a postmodernist form of social life, in which society as a whole asserts itself without bothering to ground itself" (*HL*, 43).

In his response to this criticism, Habermas did not go much beyond the position he had already taken, and while recognizing the "pluralization of diverging discourses" in the modern age (*QC*, 192),[17] he held on to the "unity of reason, even if only in a procedural sense," and to a "transcending validity claim that goes beyond merely local contexts" (*QC*, 193). Differences in opinion are expressed in the expectation of "future resolutions" (*QC*, 194). Basic for Habermas in these argumentations is the distinction "between valid and socially accepted views, between good arguments and those which are merely successful for a certain audience at a certain time" (*QC*, 194). To take a position of yes or no is more for him than to acknowledge the "claims of merely influential ideas" (*QC*,

17. Jürgen Habermas, "Questions and Counterquestions," in Bernstein, *Habermas and Modernity*, 192–216. References to this text are designated *QC*.

195). There is, rather, a basic interest for philosophy, for philosophy's role as "guardian of reason," to see social practices of justification "as more than just such practices" (*QC*, 195). While preserving for philosophy the "possibility of speaking of rationality in the singular," Habermas also wants a "concept of communicative rationality" that does not fall prey to the "totalizing and self-referential critique of reason" in the postmodern manner, be this "via Heidegger to Derrida" or "via Bataille to Foucault." He finds this type of rationality in the "everyday practice of communication" (*QC*, 196) and believes that "the socially integrative powers of the religious tradition shaken by enlightenment can find an equivalent in the unifying, consensus-creating power of reason" (*QC*, 197).

Viewed from the radical critique of reason in the postmodern manner, these arguments are of course more desirabilities, or what Habermas considers to be desirabilities, than demonstrative truths. To give these thoughts more profile, however, we should add that Habermas's "unifying, consensus-creating power of reason" is not to be taken in the sense of a stable, ideal, transcendental, or in any other way identifiable and objectifiable principle of metaphysics of presence. Communicative reason manifests itself through basic differences among the communicating partners, through endless argumentations and counter-argumentations, and leads to no enduring, everlasting result. The consensus-creating power of reason, in other words, constantly creates itself and is never fully realized. With its claim to validity, communicative reason transcends the present, but this transcendence is never absolutely accomplished and permanently renews itself. The presence of truth is indefinitely deferred. Yet in spite of all these delays and postponements, we are not yet out of Hegelianism. Reason and truth remain the centering ground and determine social discourse structurally and historically. With this model of thought, Habermas reaffirms and continues the "project of modernity" while leaving the territory of postmodernity to Rorty and others, not without warning, however, that this is a dangerous philosophical zone of performative contradictions and self-referential traps.

5

Other proponents of postmodernism see the end of modernity in organic images of aging, decay, and natural death. Jean Baudrillard describes the process as one of an immense loss of meaning leading to complete indifference, in a state where an obese growth of the same has replaced the innovative élan toward the new. "We are truly in a beyond," Baudrillard says:

> The imagination is in power, likewise the enlightenment and the intelligence, and we are experiencing now or in the near future the perfection of the social. Everything has been accomplished, the heaven of utopia has come down to earth, and what once stood out in a shining perspective, now appears as catastrophe in slow motion. We already sense the fatal taste of the material paradise. And transparency, in the age of alienation an expression of the ideal order, is fulfilled today in the form of a homogeneous and terrorist space.[18]

Gianni Vattimo sees the "end of modernity" in more academic manner as an "ontological decay," an erosion of principles such as subject, being, or truth. He attempts to provide an art of living for the late-modern and postmodern types of existence which have left behind any recourse to finality and presence, as far postponed as these consolations might ever

18. Jean Baudrillard, *Les stratégies fatales* (Paris: Grasset, 1983), 85.

be. The inspiration for this manner of existence derives from a very personally appropriated Nietzsche in the style of *Human, All Too Human* or a Heidegger understood as initiation into death.[19]

Although he does not use terms such as modernism and postmodernism, because of their determining, binding character, the style of postmodern writing and the reflective, ironic mode of postmodern thinking is performed at its best in the texts of Jacques Derrida. Here, the end of modernity, or better, the infinite transgression of modernity, is not declared by a statement but enacted through performative writing and communicated indirectly. Casual remarks such as the following are the most direct statements on postmodernism by Derrida, but altogether atypical for his style: "If modernism distinguishes itself through a striving for absolute domination, postmodernism is perhaps the statement or experience of its end, the end of this plan for domination."[20] However, one should always keep in mind that pluralism, polysemy, and difference are for Derrida no loss of unity (past history), nor a momentary lack of coherence to be overcome (future), but the character of linguisticity itself (present), and therefore attributable to all periods in history. The phenomenon of postmodernism is thereby raised to a truly theoretical and philosophical level, and the critique of reason, the decisive mark of postmodernism, is carried out, not from a temporary perspective or some disciplinary point of view, but as a genuine philosophical task.

Among the various texts by Derrida, none is perhaps more

19. Gianni Vattimo, *Al di là soggetto* (Milano: Feltrinelli, 1985) and *La fine della modernità* (Milano: Feltrinelli, 1985).

20. Jacques Derrida and Eva Meyer, "Labyrinth und Archi/Textur," in *Das Abenteuer der Ideen: Architektur und Philosophie seit der industriellen Revolution* (Berlin: Austellungskatalog, 1984), 94–106.

exemplary for his style of postmodern writing and postmodern thought than the small composition, *Of a Recently Adopted Apocalyptic Tone in Philosophy.*[21] The text cannot be reduced to the postmodern debate but certainly articulates aspects of it, although in an entirely indirect, casual manner. It is Derrida's response, his ironic account of and disarming contribution to a colloquium devoted to his work, more precisely, to his position concerning "the ends of man."[22]

The end of man is a prominent theme in contemporary thought and closely connected with the death of the subject, the disappearance of subjectivity as the last grounding principle of modernity in its desire for self-assurance. What appeared to be the final basis of our structures of knowledge, moral, social, and political activities, and aesthetic creations as well as enjoyments, that is, human reality, transcendental subjectivity, becomes involved in a bewildering sort of questioning and appears to be predetermined by supraindividual and transsubjective constellations of power. These predeterminations devaluate the seemingly primary principle of subjectivity to a completely secondary entity, an incidental effect in the discursive formation of epochs, a predetermined glance at the world which is codified by preestablished sequences in the mobile system of signs, discourses, institutions, and canons. The critical doubt that the human level might not be the ultimate reality for evaluations of a broader scope goes hand in hand with the Nietzschean impulse to leave behind the "anthropomorphic" point of view and to transcend merely humanistically based value judgments in the style of the "hu-

21. Jacques Derrida, *D'un ton apocalyptique adopté naguère en philosophie* (Paris: Editions Galilée, 1983). Translations are my own. References to this text are designated *TA*.

22. *Les fins de l'homme à partir du travail de Jacques Derrida: Colloque de Cérisy, 23 juillet–2 août 1980* (Paris: Editions Galilée, 1981).

man, all too human." It is from such considerations that Foucault formulated at the end of *The Order of Things* his famous phrase about the erasing of man who disappears "like a face drawn in the sand at the edge of the sea."[23] No other topic of postmodern thought has aroused more indignation than this proclamation of the end of man.

In a subtle configuration of the two meanings of the word end, goal and death, Derrida suggests through his title "The Ends of Man" that it might very well be the end (goal, destination, aim, term) of man to reach his end, and this again in a multiplicity of senses: his completion, his *telos,* his self-overcoming, his abolition, extinction, and death.[24] Who could deny this ultimate task? Some of the greatest philosophers of the modern age, Hegel, Husserl, Heidegger, not to mention Nietzsche, were deeply immersed in this thought but also demonstrated the inachievability of such an enterprise, the necessity and impossibility of thinking and experiencing the "end" of man. The thinking of limit and the thinking of goal always get in each other's way in such fundamental thought and reveal the more basic fact that the "name of man has always been inscribed in metaphysics between these two ends" (*EM,* 123). Indeed, Derrida continues, the end of man in this double-edged sense, has "since always" been prescribed "in the thinking and the language of Being" in the West, and "this prescription has never done anything but modulate the equivocality of the *end,* in the play of *telos* and death" (*EM,* 134). To bring this interplay to its full fruition, Derrida suggests reading the sequence in the following way by taking all words in all

23. Michel Foucault, *The Order of Things: An Archaeology of the Human Sciences* (New York: Random House, 1973), 387.

24. Jacques Derrida, "The Ends of Man," in *Margins of Philosophy,* trans. Alan Bass (Chicago: The University of Chicago Press, 1982), 109–36. References to this text are designated *EM.*

their senses: "the end of man is the thinking of Being, man is the end of the thinking of Being, the end of man is the end of the thinking of Being." As an afterthought he adds: "Man, since always, is his proper end, that is, the end of his proper. Being, since always, is its proper end, that is, the end of its proper" (*EM,* 134).

This double-edged position concerning the ends of man motivated the conference on the same theme, and when Derrida gave a speech entitled *Of a Recently Adopted Apocalyptic Tone in Philosophy,* he had to raise his irony of *telos* and *thanatos* to even higher powers, now including his own apocalyptic-eschatological tone of philosophy.[25] In its title the text is a parody of Kant's essay of 1796, "Of a Recently Adopted Superior Tone in Philosophy," where Kant protests against writers in philosophy who departed from the logical and demonstrative type of reasoning and claimed to have access to truth through a supernatural kind of revelation, through an "eschatological mystagogy." Authors whom Kant had particularly in mind were Schlosser and Jacobi. Schlosser, known for his mysticism and visionary enthusiasm, had received the name of "the new German Orpheus" from his contemporaries, and was referred to as "the ominous voice of the orphic sage."[26] Jacobi was notorious for his opposition to the speculative manner of reasoning in the style of transcendental idealism. Since he attempted to supplement philosophical speculation with an immediate revelation within the inner self, a direct and unmediated access to truth through personal intimation, his philosophy, in an anticipation of Kierkegaard, became known as

25. See Derrida, *D'un ton apocalyptique,* and *The Ends of Man.*

26. Friedrich Schlegel in his reviews of Schlosser, *Studien zur Philosophie und Theologie,* in *Kritische Friedrich Schlegel Ausgabe,* ed. Ernst Behler (Paderborn-München: Schöningh, 1975), vol. 8, 3, 33.

the "philosophy of the leap," the philosophy of the *salto,* which for some, of course, was a *salto mortale* into the abyss of divinity.[27]

It was against these authors and also against anyone else in his time who embroidered philosophy with poetry and non-rational argumentations that Kant assumed the attitude of rational enlightenment, of the "police in the realm of the sciences" (*TA,* 31), and warned against the castration, the annihilation, and the death of all true philosophy through such transgressions (*TA,* 21). Writers such as Schlosser and Jacobi put themselves outside of the community of human beings by considering themselves as privileged, as an elite, and in possession of some mysterious secret which they alone are able to reveal (*TA,* 28–29). These authors confront the "voice of reason" with the "voice of an oracle" (*TA,* 30). They believe that work is useless in philosophy and that it would suffice to lend an ear to an oracle inside oneself (*TA,* 32). Borrowing the revelatory vocabulary used by his adversaries, Kant characterizes them as "approaching the goddess of wisdom so closely that they perceive the rustling of her robe," or as "making the veil of Isis so thin that one can surmise under it the goddess" (*TA,* 44).

Without pointing it out continuously, Derrida indicates sufficiently that what Kant has to say about the "mystagogues" and the death of philosophy in his time can easily be applied to our contemporary writers on postmodernity. In a certain way, Derrida mimes Kant's text, but he also parodies it and thereby transforms, deforms it (*TA,* 17). On the one hand, he

27. Friedrich Heinrich Jacobi, "Open Letter to Fichte, 1799," and "On Faith and Knowledge in Response to Schelling and Hegel," trans. Diana I. Behler, in *Philosophy of German Idealism,* ed. Ernst Behler (New York: Continuum, 1982), 119–57.

seems to assume the attitude of one who warns us in the name of rational enlightenment against the death of all true philosophy, but on the other, he casts grave doubts on the credibility of such an endeavor. These doubts arise even from the general framework in which this story is presented, the Enlightenment. We are immediately reminded that the entire structure of the Enlightenment, of the *siècle des lumières,* rests on attempts to reveal or uncover, and that the great monument of the Enlightenment, the *Encyclopédie,* has as its frontispiece an engraving depicting the unveiling of truth. We might even think that a project as serious as that of the self-assurance of modernity might result from a desire as frivolous as the lifting of the veil of Iris. Derrida does not go into these broader aspects but stays with Kant and points out that the voice of trembling astonishment, otherwise criticized as the secret of mystagogues, also animates Kant's moral law (*TA,* 36), that his entire discourse, perhaps every discourse, is located on either side, that of the Enlightenment and that of mystagogy, and that this also applies to our own modernity (*TA,* 53).

Like Kant, Derrida seems to assume the task of demystifying the grandseigneurial tone of an approaching end and to maintain the vigilant attitude of rational enlightenment. He seems to be inspired by a "desire of clarity and revelation to demystify or, if you prefer, to deconstruct the apocalyptic discourse itself, and together with it, everything that speculates about vision, imminence of the end, theophany, parousia, and final judgment" (*TA,* 64–65). Yet such deconstruction has to mobilize a great number and variety of interpretative devices and never functions without a second step, which in this case, gets involved in the finest particularities of the apocalyptic tone itself (*TA,* 66). Concentrating on St. John's *Apocalypse,* the prototype of any apocalyptical discourse, Derrida discovers one essential feature of such texts: "One no longer knows very well who in the *Apocalypse* lends his voice and tone to someone else, one no longer knows very well who addresses what to whom" (*TA*, 77). It is by no means certain that the human being is the "terminal of this endless computer." However, the question arises whether this "angelic structure," this reference to other references without decidable origin and destination, is not the scene of writing in general. Derrida asks, "Is the apocalyptic not a transcendental condition of every discourse, even of every experience, of every mark or of every trace?" (*TA*, 77–78). The task of demystifying thereby reveals itself as twofold. On the one hand, it is a task in the style of the Enlightenment and as such without limits (*TA*, 81). On the other, demystification in the style of deconstruction remains open to features in the apocalyptic discourse that transcend the realm of ontological, grammatical, linguistic, or semantic knowledge (*TA*, 93).

This realm opens up, for instance, in the apocalyptic "Come" (*erkhou, veni*) which neither comes from nor addresses itself to an identifiable, verifiable, decidable, or derivable determination. And it is here that we gather the "truth" about the apocalypse: "an apocalypse without apocalypse; an apocalypse without vision, without truth, without revelation, dispatches (because the 'Come' is plural in itself), addresses without message and destination, without decidable sender or receiver . . ." (*TA*, 95). To put it more pointedly, there is no chance for a type of thinking that wants to reveal a final truth in a final discourse of revelation. But what about the "truth" of this truth, the "truth" about the apocalypse? It is precisely here, at the breaching of the limits of communication, that postmodern thinking and writing begin to operate through circumlocution, indirectness, configuration, and ironic communication.

2

The Rise of Literary Modernism in the Romantic Age

The spirit of modernity appears to be inseparable from the idea of scientific progress forcefully instituted in the seventeenth century by Bacon, Descartes, and Pascal. For Bacon, such inventions and discoveries in the realm of the mechanical arts as gunpowder, the compass, and the art of printing had brought about so many changes in the horizon of the earth that the present had advanced to a position which in comparison to the ancients was new. Since the present could not legitimately be derived from the tradition, the authority of the tradition was suspended, making truth a daughter of time and not of authority.[1] As can be noticed, the spirit of modernity originally implied a strong expression of self-manifestation against the overwhelming and preponderant authority of the ancients. This self-assurance, however, succeeded first and most easily in the sciences.

When Pascal wrote the Preface to his treatise on empty space in 1647, he had already left behind his early veneration of the ancients and readily abandoned such scientific principles as the *horror vacui*, the fear of emptiness, when evidence and experiment convinced him.[2] He no longer considered the results of the ancients as goals of his study but as means to overcome the past, and he believed that scientific knowledge

1. Francis Bacon, *Novum Organon*, ed. Thomas Fowler (Oxford: Clarendon Press, 1899).

2. Blaise Pascal, *Oeuvres complètes* (Paris: Gallimard, 1956). References to this text are designated *BP*.

was susceptible to constant growth and infinite perfection (*BP*, 532–34). Yet the idea of progress and perfectibility articulated in this treatise only relates to the sciences in the strict sense of the term as they are based on reason and experiment (geometry, arithmetic, music, physics, and medicine), and not to those investigations that have recourse to memory and authority (history, geography, jurisprudence, linguistics, and theology). Whereas knowledge of this latter type of investigation is limited and can be perfected, the sciences can continuously be augmented and are perfectible without limit (*BP*, 529–31). It was only with regard to the sciences that Pascal enjoyed an ascendancy over the ancients and assured his contemporaries: "Our view is more extended . . . we see more than they" (*BP*, 532).

The restriction of progress and modernity was even more pronounced with regard to the arts, to literature and poetry, to the products of the imagination and subjects of taste. Progression and perfectibility remained the privilege of philosophy, the sciences, and technology and were excluded from the realm of the arts. Not until late in the eighteenth century did the ideas of progression and perfectibility enter the aesthetic domain. With regard to the historical status of the sciences and the arts, the realms of reason and imagination, European classicism and the Enlightenment show a characteristic antagonism. The sciences appeared to be involved in an interminable progression, whereas the arts were thought of as always returning in cyclical motion to that position of correct standards and appropriate norms from which they had departed in periods of decay and barbarism.

The obvious philosophical principle for this assumption was the belief that philosophy and the sciences are as infinite as truth and nature, whereas poetry and the arts have a certain point of perfection, determined by man's invariable nature, beyond which they cannot go. In this sense, we read in the *Encyclopédie*, "The fundamental rules of taste are the same in all ages because they derive from invariable attributes of the human mind."[3] Not until this principle was abandoned and the arts, like the sciences, were included in a process of infinite progression, can we speak of modernity in the full sense of the term and realize all the consequences and problems which this new situation involved.

1

It therefore appears plausible to draw the historical demarcation line for a fully developed sense of modernism at that period in Western history when, at the beginning of the romantic age and toward the end of the eighteenth century, poetry, literature, and the arts were for the first time in human history seen in a process of constant progression. This appears to be the most decisive suspension of the classical doctrine and the most impressive manifestation of the modern consciousness. Whereas the classical concept of a cyclical movement in literary history and in art history limited the production of poetry to an unsurpassable point of perfection, the notion of perfectibility set the course of poetry free for ever new creations. As one can easily realize, all decisive features of the new concept of poetry are intimately related to the notion of infinite perfectibility: the view of poetry as a creative instead of an imitative expression, the poet's genius and imagination, and the suspension of a hierarchical system of genres for the sake of a historically changing and developing one. Even the reader's act of understanding literature

3. *Encyclopédie ou dictionnaire raisonné des Sciences, des Arts et des Métiers, par une Société de Gens de Lettres* (Geneva: Pellet, 1777), vol. 2, 608–11.

became involved in the process of infinite perfectibility. This decisive step took place in various European nations at about the same time. Now the struggle between the ancients and the moderns appeared to have been won in poetry also in favor of the moderns, and the age of modernity seemed to have truly begun.

Many events in other realms of human history seem to corroborate this caesura. The most obvious is the French Revolution of 1789, which constitutes a crucial turning point in Europe's social and political life and is intimately linked with the inception of romanticism, a movement of fundamental change in literature and a radical break with the classicist tradition. For many critics, romanticism is only another expression of that radical upheaval occurring toward the end of the eighteenth century of which the French Revolution is the most conspicuous manifestation in the realm of politics and society. Philosophy could be added as further evidence for an entirely new orientation at this time. Kant, in the Preface to the second edition of his *Critique of Pure Reason* of 1787, characterized the new manner of philosophical speculation introduced by him as a Copernican turn in philosophy, namely, as a switch of perspective from the objects of perception to the perceiving subject.[4] Students of his doctrine soon declared Kant's innovation a revolution in philosophy and saw in his thought a correspondence to the French Revolution, a different expression of the general upheaval characterizing their time. The late eighteenth century thus appears to be marked by at least three revolutions, that is, in politics, in literature, and in philosophy, which in each case overcame an old order, an ancient regime, for a modern state of affairs.

4. Immanuel Kant, *Philosophical Writings*, ed. Ernst Behler, foreword by René Wellek (New York: Continuum, 1986), 6–7.

Yet there is a fundamental resistance on the part of the representatives of the arts and of poetry to take their positions unreservedly on the side of modernity. We notice a similar reluctance on the part of the historian to come to a clear-cut period designation of modernism. Even with so many indications and contemporary testimonies for an epochal break, we encounter a basic hesitancy to give the beginning of modernism a precise date. On the one hand, we feel inclined to postpone the true appearance of modernism until a time of an even fuller expression of its nature. Following this inclination, we move up the date of a beginning of modernism from the seventeenth century, its scientific manifestation, to the end of the eighteenth, to modern revolutions in different spheres of life; from there to the end of the nineteenth century, to the awakening of an increased critique and self-criticism of the modern mind; and then perhaps to our own position toward the end of the twentieth century when the rise of a "postmodern" attitude can very well be interpreted as the culmination of the modern spirit. In an opposite tendency, however, we are disposed to advance the beginning of modernism to ever earlier periods. If we recognize the appearance of a modern attitude in the new scientific self-consciousness of European rationalism, we could cite with equal reason the Reformation for such a new beginning, or the innovation brought about by the Renaissance, even the eschatological expectations connected with the year 1200, or maybe the departure from the ancient world through the rise of Christianity.

Skepticism toward neat datings of epochal breaks is also nourished by the experience of a lack of correspondence among all the cultural spheres in such events. What we encounter in history is rather a discontinuity and plurality among developments in different realms of life such as science, religion, philosophy, politics, literature, and the arts. It is with all these sceptical reservations that the attempt will be made to look at one particular phase and one particular sphere in the development of the modern mentality more closely: romanticism, more specifically, in the sphere of literature and critical theory. The ambivalent attitude toward modernism and modernity seems to appear in literature and critical thought more acutely than in any other of the cultural branches.

2

The first signs of a reversal in the enormous preponderance of the classical Greeks and Romans over the modern Europeans in the realms of literature, poetry, and artistic creation can be noticed in the so-called *querelle des anciens et des modernes,* the famous quarrel between the ancients and the moderns, between the proponents of classical art and the advocates of a modern style. This was a prominent critical debate in seventeenth- and eighteenth-century Europe, conducted mostly in France and England, later also in Germany, and truly fundamental for the formation of a modern consciousness and a pronounced sense of literary modernity. Inspired by the greatness of the Age of Louis XIV and the excellence of its poets Racine and Corneille, or convinced of the unique dramatic talent of Shakespeare, critics such as Saint-Evremond and Perrault, or Dryden, Pope, and Johnson, attempted to shake off the overwhelming weight of the classical Greek and Roman models and give the modern age self-confidence and the right to have its own style. Now people attempted to demonstrate that the modern age had not only grown beyond Aristotle's *Physics* but had also created artistic beauties unknown to the philosopher's *Poetics.* Now the ideas of progression and perfectibility, utilized so far mainly in philosophy and the sciences, were also considered for poetry and the arts. However, in contrast to the sciences, for which the idea of progress was a well-established category at that time, the realm of literature and the arts or that of imagination and taste remained determined by the notion of an unchangeable human nature until far into the eighteenth century.

This ambiguous feeling is obvious even among the proponents of the moderns in this quarrel and seems to express a basic resistance among literary authors and literary critics to being outspokenly and deliberately promodern. A promodern attitude appeared to imply an anti-ancient or anticlassical stance, and spokesmen for the modern attitude attempted to circumvent this impression by giving their argument a configurative structure, a double meaning, and an ambiguous expression. Fontenelle is a case in point for this double-edged modernity. In *A Digression on the Ancients and the Moderns* of 1688, he claims that the whole question of the preeminence of the ancients and moderns boils down "to knowing whether the trees which used to be seen in the countryside were taller than those of today" and thinks that "if our trees are as tall as those of former times, then we can equal Homer, Plato, and Demosthenes" (*DAM,* 358).[5] For if the ancients were in a more advantageous position than we, he argues, then "brains in those days were better arranged," just as trees would have been taller and more beautiful. In reality, however, "nature has at hand a certain clay which is always the same." Yet while centuries do not put "any natural differences among men," different climates do, as well as other exterior circumstances, and this is obvious in the different characters of nations (*DAM,* 360).

5. Bernard Le Bouvier de Fontenelle, *A Digression on the Ancients and the Moderns,* in *The Continental Model,* ed. Scott Elledge and Donald Schier (Ithaca: Cornell University Press, 1970). References to this text are designated *DAM.*

In contrast to the sciences and philosophy, eloquence and poetry require only a limited number of ideas for Fontenelle and depend primarily on the imagination. Perfection in these arts can therefore be achieved "in a few centuries" (*DAM,* 363). Once we have decided that the ancients have reached the point of perfection and cannot be surpassed, however, we should not conclude from there that "they cannot be equaled" (*DAM,* 365). Such equality, however, is not easy to measure. The Greeks when compared to the Romans seem inferior, just as the Romans are more modern compared to the Greeks (*DAM,* 364). Humanity appears as a living being that will never age (*DAM,* 366–67). One day, Fontenelle argues, his own time, the Age of Louis XIV, will become contemporary with the Greeks and the Romans, that is, ancient (*DAM,* 368). If the great men of this century had charitable feelings toward posterity, he recommends, "they would warn later ages not to admire them too much" (*DAM,* 369). Fontenelle, in other words, although a modern, is convinced of a basic equality existing between the ancients and the moderns (*DAM,* 360) and says: "I should like to paint Nature with scales in her hand, like Justice, to indicate how she weighs and measures out almost equally whatever she distributes among men, happiness, talent, the advantages and disadvantages of different social stations, the facilities and difficulties associated with the things of the mind" (*DAM,* 368).

The best example of such refined and complex modernism in the English version of the quarrel between the ancients and the moderns is perhaps Dryden's *Essay of Dramatic Poesy* (1668, revised in 1684).[6] Four witty and civilized interlocutors, while drifting down the river Thames in a barge, engage in a critical discussion which soon focuses on the difference between the

6. *Essays of John Dryden,* ed. W. P. Ker (New York: Russell and Russell, 1961). References to this text are designated *DP.*

ancients and the moderns in the field of drama and includes not only the French theater but also the development of English drama from Beaumont, Fletcher, and Jonson to Shakespeare. Among the discussion partners we soon discover the voice of Dryden (Neander). He sees in Shakespeare's dramas a new spirit of literature no longer based on rules and decorum but on fullness of life, humor, passion, and "wit," and praises Shakespeare as "the Homer, or father of our dramatic poets." Yet when they land at Somerset Stairs and the four friends come to shore, they have not agreed on anything, but everybody has had his say and reply and shown his openness to opposite arguments. Dryden later emphasized the sceptical, ironic mood animating this conversation by referring to the manner of argumentation in Plato's dialogues. He said, "My whole discourse was sceptical, according to that way of reasoning which was used by Socrates, Plato, and all the Academics of old," and he added, "You see it is a dialogue sustained by persons of several opinions, all of them left doubtful, to be determined by the readers in general" (*DP*, 124).

The feeling of superiority over the ancients can more easily be discovered among critics in the field of tragedy. Perrault, for instance, gave unreserved preference to the tragedies of Corneille and Racine over those of the Greeks. The ancients, he argued, knew the seven planets and the great number of the fixed stars, as his own time did, but not the satellites of the planets or the great number of the small stars discovered since (*PAM* 2:29–30).[7] Similarly, they knew "the passions of the soul, but not the affinity of small affections and small circumstances which accompany them." As anatomy had dis-

7. Charles Perrault, *Parallèle des Anciens et des Modernes en ce qui regarde les arts and les sciences,* ed. Hans Robert Jauβ (Munich: Kindler, 1964). References to this text are designated *PAM*.

covered new facts about the human heart that had escaped the knowledge of the ancients, so moral knowledge had come to include inclinations, aversions, desires, and disgusts of which the ancients had no idea. Perrault believed it was possible to point out in the works of the authors of his time—in their moral treatises, their tragedies, their novels, and their rhetorical writings—thousands of delicate sentiments entirely absent in the ancients (*PAM*, 2:30–31).

This is a basic line of argumentation in seventeenth-century criticism intimately related to the literary discourse of modernity. Saint-Evremond, perhaps the most outspoken partisan of the moderns in this debate about tragedy, declared in his *Of Ancient and Modern Tragedy* (1672) that Aristotle's *Poetics* was as outdated as his *Physics*. Just as Descartes and Gassendi had discovered truths that were unknown to Aristotle, so Corneille had created "beauties for the stage of which Aristotle was ignorant" (*AMT*, 171).[8] He believed that if the best works of antiquity in this genre—*Oedipus Rex*, for example—were translated into French with the same force as the original, we would realize "that nothing in the world would appear to us more cruel, more opposed to the true sentiments mankind ought to have" (*AMT*, 182). Fontenelle maintained in his *Digression on the Ancients and the Moderns* of 1688 that the best works of Sophocles, Euripides, or Aristophanes would not stand up to the tragedies and comedies of the Age of Louis XIV and that "nothing so limits progress, nothing narrows the mind so much as excessive admiration of the ancients" (*DAM*, 368–69). Even Boileau, the leading partisan of the

8. Charles de Saint-Evremond, *Oeuvres en prose*, ed. René Ternois (Paris: Didier, 1969), vol. 4, 170–84. The translation is taken from Pierre Desmaizeauz, *The Works of M. de Saint-Evremond* (London, 1928), available in Scott Elledge and Donald Schier, eds., *The Continental Model* (Ithaca: Cornell University Press, 1970), 123–30. References to this text are designated *AMT*.

ancients, admitted that the Age of Louis XIV had seen innovations in dramatic art unknown to Aristotle, but he asked Perrault, his main adversary in this dispute, rhetorically, whether he could deny "that it is from Livy, from Dio Cassius, from Plutarch, from Lucan, and Seneca that M. de Corneille took his finest touches," or "that it is Sophocles and Euripides who made M. de Racine," or "that it is in Plautus and Terence that Molière learned the greatest niceties of his art."[9]

The belief in a distinct superiority of French classical tragedy increased considerably during the eighteenth century. In his *Dissertation on Ancient and Modern Tragedy* of 1748, Voltaire declared that it would reveal a great lack of judgment if one did not realize "how much the French stage surpasses the Greek by virtue of the art of performance, by invention, and by countless particular beauties." By substituting history for Greek mythology and by introducing politics, ambition, jealousy, and the passions of love as dominant elements in the theater, French tragedy achieved a much more truthful imitation of nature for Voltaire.[10] Another important distinction between ancient and modern tragedy can be found in Diderot's *Encyclopedia* of 1751–72. Taking up an idea already developed in Fontenelle's *Reflexions on Poetics* (1742), the author of the article on tragedy classifies the genre according to two different sources of misfortune, one outside of ourselves and the other internal (*E*, 33:840).[11] Ancient tragedy is described as based exclusively on extraneous causes: "destiny,

9. Nicolas Boileau-Despréaux, *Oeuvres complètes* (Paris: Gallimard, 1966). The translations are taken from Boileau, *Selected Criticism*, trans. Ernest Dilworth (Indianapolis: The Library of Liberal Arts, 1965), 55.

10. Published as preface to his tragedy *Sémiramis* (1748). Quoted from *Oeuvres complètes de Voltaire* (Kehl: De l'Imprimerie de la Société Littéraire Typographique, 1785), vol. 3, 357–91.

11. *Encyclopédie* (Geneva: Pellet, 1772), vol. 33, where the article is attributed to Jean-François Marmontel. References to this text are designated *E*.

the anger of the gods or their will without any motivation—in a word, fate" (*E*, 33:841). In the modern system, tragedy is no longer a picture of the calamities of the human being as a slave of fate, but of his own passions. The nucleus of tragic action has been placed in the human heart. This at least is the case of the modern tragedy created by Corneille. After the renaissance of letters, it was he who discovered a new source of tragic events sharply different from the fabulous history to which Greek tragedy was bound. And with this discovery, "modern Europe recognized the type of tragedy that was its own" (*E*, 33:845).

Yet even those who clearly assumed the superiority of the moderns over the ancients in literature and poetry refused to apply the ideas of progress and perfectibility to this realm. The reason for their reluctance was simply that they no longer saw themselves as part of the great flowering of literature and the arts which had marked the Age of Louis XIV, but already on the side of a descent from this point of perfection. The cause for this decline, however, was attributed to "the growth of reason at the expense of imagination."[12] Perrault realized this development with the thought, pleasant to him, "that there are not likely many things to be envied from those who will come after us" (*PAM*, 1:99). Voltaire called the Age of Louis XIV the "age of genius," in comparison to which "the present century merely reasons about genius."[13] Diderot saw himself as a poet for whom philosophy had cut the strings of his lyre.[14] In the *Salon* of 1767, he wrote: "The old roads

12. See on this René Wellek, "The Price of Progress in Eighteenth-Century Reflections on Literature," *Studies on Voltaire and the Eighteenth Century* 151–55 (1976), 2265–84.

13. Voltaire, "Défense du siècle de Louis XIV," *Oeuvres complètes*, ed. Louis Moland, 52 vols. (Paris: Garnier, 1877–85), vol. 28, 338.

14. Frans Hemsterhuis, *Lettre sur l'homme et ses rapports: Avec le commentaire*

are occupied by sublime models which one despairs of equalling. One writes poetics; one invents new genres; one becomes singular, bizarre, mannered."[15] Such considerations were accompanied by speculations about the origin of language according to which the first stages in an imagined genesis of language were concrete, metaphorical, and poetic, but the following ones colorless, artificial, abstract, and philosophical.

The wittiest and most playful treatment of the subject is perhaps David Hume's essay of 1755, *Of the Rise and the Progress of the Arts and the Sciences.*[16] In this discussion of progress, Hume links the arts with the sciences and ironically intends to raise their communal status from a merely natural and cyclical development to one of reason and progression. He couches this intention in the question of whether it is from "chance" or from "causes" that the rise and the progress of the arts and the sciences can be derived, implying of course that "what is owing to chance" is incomprehensible and natural, whereas "what proceeds from causes" is reasonable and intelligible. The seemingly firm basis for the progress and perfectibility of the arts and the sciences established by Hume evaporates, however, as soon as such progress is inspected more closely. This becomes apparent in the four principles of his essay formulated as "observations." His first observation is "That it is impossible for the arts and sciences to arise, at first, among any people, unless that people enjoy the blessing of a free government" (*R,* 66). The next observation strengthens this point and states "That nothing is more favourable to the

inédit de Diderot, ed. Georges May (New Haven: Yale University Press, 1964), 85.

15. Denis Diderot, *Salon* (1767), ed. Jean Sznec and Jean Adhémar, 3 (1767) (Oxford: Oxford University Press, 1963), vol. 3, 336.

16. David Hume, *Essays, Literary, Moral and Political* (London: Ward, Lock, and Co., n.d.), 63–79. References to this text are designated *R.*

rise of politeness and learning, than a number of neighbouring and independent states, connected together by commerce and policy" (*R*, 68). The third, however, encounters some difficulty in the uniformity of progress, in that "a republic is most favourable to the growth of the sciences, and a civilized monarchy to that of the polite arts" (*R*, 71). The fourth, finally, formulates the impasse progress and progressivity run into and announces "That when the arts and sciences came to perfection in any state, from that moment they naturally or rather necessarily decline, and seldom or never revive in that nation, where they formerly flourished" (*R*, 78).

3

It therefore appears to be obvious that an entirely new concept of poetry and a fundamentally new sense of modernity had to emerge when the classical model of literary creation was overcome and replaced by a notion of poetry involved in a process of infinite progression. This decisive step took place in various European nations at about the same time and marks the beginning of romanticism. Applying infinite perfectibility to the arts, these writers created an entirely new concept of the literary text participating in the progress of ideas and standing in the liveliest exchange with social life in which literature participates. Indeed, if we were to describe the specific character of that literary modernity which manifested itself toward the end of the eighteenth century in European romanticism, we would presumably come to the conclusion that it was the readiness to assume for art, particularly for poetry, an unlimited changeability and mutability.

Infinite perfectibility is also an expression of the reaction to the French Revolution of these early romantics. In this sense the idea of an infinite perfectibility appears in their writings as a somewhat confused explanation, a bewildered exclamation, or an apologetic response uttered by those who had invested all their expectations in the Revolution, were startled by its unforeseen course, and now attempted to make sense of a sequence of events that seemed to contradict perfectibility. In a curious twist, the idea that had been a motivating force for the revolutionary consciousness was put at the end, postponed as the last consolation or justification, since the Revolution failed or appeared to have failed. This attitude is closely connected with the attempt to consider the French Revolution a lost cause but to rescue its treasure, the liberation of humanity, through means other than political ones, and perhaps also more efficient and lasting than political ones. This transformation of the Revolution into a universal and philosophical emancipation of humanity is a dominant attempt by the romantics in all European countries of that time and explains basic features of the literary modernity manifesting itself in the romantic age. Here we are at the beginning of critical reflections about the French Revolution which constitute perhaps the most important response to this event. These reflections are inseparable from the spirit of modernity as it arose during the romantic age and from the notion of an infinite perfectibility of the human race. Yet this notion is quite distinct from its particular expression during the eighteenth century. Infinite perfectibility and the experience of modernism were at that time combined with a feeling of loss, with melancholy, irony, and regret, with an attitude of "in spite of," that is, with sentiments contradicting the confident expectations of the Enlightenment but forming an integral part of the romantic mentality.

As far as the outbreak of the Revolution is concerned, Madame de Staël, although still very young at that time, was perhaps better positioned than anybody else for disentangling the various causes of this event. Her most direct account of it certainly is her *Considerations of the French Revolution,*[17] but in a broader sense her entire oeuvre can be regarded as a response to the Revolution. The text, however, that in the most immediate sense attempts to provide a perspective for a comprehension of the Revolution is her *On Literature* of 1800, which indeed has as its central theme the perfectibility of the human mind.[18] In spite of all its obvious shortcomings in historical scholarship, the book is quite revolutionary in its program and in this regard corresponds to the event for which it formulates an answer. To view literature from the perspective of perfectibility was without any doubt a decisive suspension of the classical doctrine and an impressive manifestation of the forthcoming romantic revolution. With this theory, Madame de Staël had not only declared herself a partisan of the moderns in the quarrel between the ancients and the moderns, but also revealed essential new features in the appreciation of modern literature. These consisted in a cultivation of the gentler passions of the soul, a more subtle knowledge of the intricacies of the human heart, the esteem of women in human relationships, and a profound interaction of literature with the philosophy and social institutions of its time. If one compared the authors of the seventeenth century, mostly occupied with "les plaisirs de l'esprit" (*OL,* 271), to those of the eighteenth, Madame de Staël thought, one could see an anticipation of the great change which political freedom could produce in literature, and the question would

17. Madame de Staël, *Considérations sur la Révolution française,* ed. Jacques Godechot (Paris: Tallandier, 1983). References to this text are designated *CRF.*

18. Madame de Staël, *De la littérature considérée dans ses rapports avec les institutions sociales,* ed., Paul van Tieghem (Geneva and Paris: Droz, 1959). References to this text are designated *OL.*

come to mind: "But what power could talent acquire within a government where the mind is a real force?" (*OL,* 288).

It is precisely on this question that the second part of *On Literature* concentrates. After having introduced the French Revolution "as a new era in the intellectual world," Madame de Staël pursues the problem of what "the character of the literature of a great nation, an enlightened nation, where liberty and political equality are established and morals are in accordance with its institutions" would be (*OL,* 291). To be more precise, Madame de Staël fully realized that as "the vulgarity of language, of manners, of opinions" testify, the Revolution had in many regards brought about a retrogradation of taste and reason (*OL,* 293). As far as the terror is concerned, she suggests considering this horrible time "as completely outside of the circle which the events of life circumscribe, as a monstrous phenomenon which nothing regular either explains or produces" (*OL,* 293). Her *Considerations of the French Revolution* depicts the crimes of that time in images which have become famous. Concerning the period following the proscription of the Gironde, 31 May 1793, she writes, "It seems as if one descends like Dante from circle to circle ever more deeply into hell," and says about the reign of terror in general, "The facts become confused in this epoch, and one fears not being able to enter such a history without having the imagination preserve ineffaceable traces of blood" (*CRF,* 303). What frightened her most in remembering these events was perhaps not so much that eighty people were executed daily for a period of about twenty months, but that all the while, the inhabitants of Paris pursued their daily routines as if nothing were happening, so that "all the insipidness and all the frivolity of life continued alongside the most somber furies" (*CRF,* 306–7). Yet, perfectibility in literature and philosophy cannot in the long run be impeded by these events. Madame de Staël says, "The new progresses in literature and philosophy which I will indicate continue the system of perfectibility, the march of which I have traced since the Greeks" (*OL,* 294).

Madame de Staël's *On Literature* seems to be the first delineation of perfectibility and modernity in the domain of literature with all the consequences such a theory implies. Yet if we concentrate on the accomplishments gained through literary perfectibility and described by Madame de Staël as the acquisition of a new sensibility and a more thorough knowledge of the human heart, we realize a profoundly ambiguous appreciation of that literary modernity which is now arising. For these accomplishments consist in features such as "the fear of death, the yearning for life, the devotion without limit" (*OL,* 150). Ancient poetry, to use the later distinctions between classicism and romanticism, is that of a full identity with itself, or self-presence, perfect integrality, and a harmonious display of poetic power and joy in life. Modern poetry is that of longing, nonidentity, otherness, reflection, dissimulation, and melancholy.[19] With regard to a more recent period of literature, French classicism, Madame de Staël admits that the Age of Louis XIV was "the most remarkable of all in literature," and the author who had reached the highest point of perfection was undoubtedly Racine (*OL,* 224). Racine's and Fénelon's aesthetic qualities could not be surpassed. To be sure, Voltaire combined the grace of the previous century with the philosophy of his own and knew how "to embellish the charm of the spirit with all those truths from which one did not yet think an application possible" (*OL,* 281). This was by no means an unconditional praise of literary modernity, however, but

19. Madame de Staël, *De l'Allemagne: Nouvelle édition par la Comtesse Jean de Pange avec le concours de Simone Balayé.* 2 vols. (Paris: Hachette, 1958–60), vol. 2, 211–15.

rather an admission that the time for the pure beauty of classicism was gone. When her adversaries reproached Madame de Staël for having violated the principles of classicism by applying the notion of perfectibility to poetry, she replied that her subject had not been that which belongs purely to the arts of the imagination, but the art of literature including reflection and philosophy, and that one could never determine an end where thought would stop (*OL*, 9–10).

In a now famous study, Jean Starobinski saw one of the secret bonds between Madame de Staël's life and her oeuvre, her own character and that of her heroines, in a profound ambiguity and double evaluation as far as their involvement in life was concerned. On the one hand, out of an inner richness, there is the overflowing desire to dissipate and to communicate in an expansive, future-oriented movement, but on the other, there is the reciprocal "feeling of incompleteness" resulting in resignation and melancholy.[20] This is not the occasion for following Starobinski into his subtle analyses of Madame de Staël's writings from the points of view of "suicide moral" and "morte-vivante," as enticing as this approach might appear for an interpretation of her conceptions of literary classicism and modernism. But one can say on this basis that double reaction and double evaluation characterize not only Madame de Staël's fictional writings, but also her theory of writing as it is centered in her belief in perfectibility and modernity in literature.

4

The early representatives of English romanticism, the members of the Lake School, responded to the French Rev-

20. Jean Starobinski, "Suicide et mélancolie chez Mme de Staël," in *Madame de Staël et l'Europe: Colloque de Coppet* (Paris: Klincksieck, 1970), 242–52.

olution with genuine enthusiasm. In the sixth book of *The Prelude,* describing his first trip to France in the summer of 1790 with his friend Robert Jones, Wordsworth rejoiced on the first anniversary of the Revolution in the experience of a time "when joy of one is joy of tens of millions" (6:346).[21] He and his friend were drawn into the general emotion of fraternity because, as Wordsworth said, "We bore a name Honour'd in France, the name of Englishmen" (6:408). Many people felt that France was catching up with England's "glorious revolution" of 1688 and heading for a constitutional monarchy. There are several books and articles of the time that claimed to grasp the "spirit of the age," all coming to the same conclusion, namely, that the literary innovations of that period received their main stimulus from the French Revolution. This applies especially to the years prior to the turn from the eighteenth to the nineteenth century. According to William Hazlitt, the entire Lake School of poetry "had its origin in the French Revolution, or rather in those sentiments and opinions which produced the Revolution." He considered Wordsworth's *Lyrical Ballads* as mirroring "the revolutionary movement of our age" and said about its author, "the political changes of the day were the model on which he formed and conducted his poetical experiments."[22]

This feeling was originally kindled by the notion of infinite perfectibility as promulgated in Godwin's *Enquiry Concerning Political Justice.* Yet the revolutionary spirit in English romanticism was strongly connected with a religious perspective. Some of the English romantics were Unitarians or Dissidents,

21. William Wordsworth, *The Prelude,* ed. Stephen Parrish (Ithaca: Cornell University Press, 1977). References to this poem are given directly in the text.

22. William Hazlitt, "The Spirit of the Age," in *William Hazlitt: The Collected Works,* ed. A. R. Waller and Arnold Glover (London: Dent, 1902), vol. 4, 271.

and Wordsworth and Coleridge were preparing for the clergy before the turn of the century. The renovation of the earth and the regeneration of the human race assumed Christian or biblical dimensions and were often expressed in visionary, apocalyptic, or mythical images reminiscent of Blake's *The French Revolution* of 1791 and Milton's prophetic attitudes. This is still obvious in Coleridge's visionary poem *The Destiny of Nations* (1796), depicting "The Progress of Liberty" through the "vision of the Maid of Orleans."[23] Wordsworth concluded the *Descriptive Sketches* of 1793 with the prophecy of a new earth emerging from apocalyptic fires and a return to a golden age.[24] When, with the beginning of the Reign of Terror, the public mood in England suddenly shifted, Godwin, according to Hazlitt, "sunk below the horizon" and the reputation of his *Enquiry* along with him.[25] Coleridge tried to water down his early revolutionary fervor and later completely dissociated himself from this attitude. Wordsworth tried to justify the terror with world historical considerations, and in *A Letter to the Bishop of Llandaff* argued with revolutionary logic against the bishop, Dr. Richard Watson, who had supported the Revolution in its early days but publicly recanted after the execution of Louis XVI: "What! have you so little knowledge of the nature of man as to be ignorant, that a time of revolution is not the season of true Liberty. Alas! the obstinacy and perversion of men is such that she is too often obliged to borrow the very arms of despotism to overthrow him, and in order to reign in peace must establish herself in

23. *The Complete Poetical Works of Samuel Taylor Coleridge,* ed. E. H. Coleridge (Oxford: Clarendon, 1912), vol. 1, 131.

24. *William Wordsworth, Poetical Works,* ed. F. Selincourt and H. Darbishire, 5 vols. (Oxford: Oxford University Press, 1940–49), vol. 1, 42–91.

25. Hazlitt, *The Collected Works,* vol. 4, 201.

violence."[26] As he formulated it later in *The Prelude,* Wordsworth did not lay the blame for the Reign of Terror at the door of the Revolution itself but on

> a reservoir of guilt
> And ignorance, fill'd up from age to age,
> That could no longer hold its loathsome charge,
> But burst and spread in deluge through the land.
> (10:437–40)

Yet Hazlitt's observation about the origin of early English romantic poetry in the sentiments and opinions produced by the French Revolution holds true even for the period after this revolutionary fervor had disappeared and vanished under the impact of the Reign of Terror and the disappointing subsequent course of the Revolution. As M. H. Abrams has shown, the great romantic poems "were written not in the mood of revolutionary exaltation but in the later mood of revolutionary disillusionment and despair."[27] The revolutionary theme in English romanticism thereby assumed a profoundly poetic nature, a genuinely lyrical expression. After the apocalyptic expectations for a general renewal of man and nature had been shattered, the poetic mind attempted to preserve the lost treasure of the Revolution by shaping it as hope for universal regeneration, or the poetic mind shifted from an abstract anticipation of apocalyptic change in the history of mankind to the reality of hope for the everyday life of the individual, as in Wordsworth's *Lyrical Ballads* and other poetry written after his estrangement from the French Revolu-

26. *The Selected Prose and Poetry of Wordsworth,* ed. Geoffrey H. Hartman (New York: Meridian, 1980), 43–44.

27. M. H. Abrams, "English Romanticism: The Spirit of the Age," in *Romanticism and Consciousness: Essays in Criticism,* ed. Harold Bloom (New York: Norton, 1970), 91–119.

tion, in 1794. This lyrical mood, in its withdrawal from a celebration of the French Revolution but maintenance of hope for a general redemption of humanity, seems to correspond to the double-edged affirmation of perfectibility and literary modernity in European romanticism in the sense of both scepticism toward any achievable final goal and belief in the pursuit of such a goal. Another way Wordsworth maintained the theme of the French Revolution in spite of his later scepticism toward it was to integrate this event, as well as his early participation in it, with his autobiography. Here again, a subtle double gesture is exercised with regard to a period of life which has become problematical but still maintains its existence in the framework of autobiography. Although at the time of the composition of *The Prelude,* consideration of his revolutionary phase was for Wordsworth, as he put it, a look on "painful things," he nevertheless considered this period important for himself and integrated it with the autobiographical structure of the "growth of a poet's mind," thereby affirming it in the context of his life.

5

If we wanted to determine the special style of the new poetic and critical discourse brought about by the early romantic authors, we would have to abandon the dominance of one single principle (reason, creative imagination, structure, progress, perfectibility, and so forth) and stress the counteractive movement of several tendencies (affirmation and scepticism, enthusiasm and melancholy) as the characteristic mark of their discourse. With regard to the modernity of the romantic attitude, we would have to add that it implies a critique of any straightforward type of modernism, of a modernism that lacks self-critical assessment of its own position and an awareness of the deficiencies it implies.

Friedrich Schlegel is perhaps the best representative for such self-reflective modernism in German romanticism. In a fragment written in 1798, hardly a page long, he characterized his concept of modern or, as he preferred to say, romantic poetry and, like Madame de Staël, demanded that this poetry be "in touch with philosophy and rhetoric" and interact with life making "poetry lively and sociable, and life and society poetical" (*FS,* 2:182–83; *LF,* 175).[28] The fusion of poetry and philosophy also has for Schlegel the meaning of a "poetic reflection," inseparable from the creative process, animating the entire poetic work, and blending the author's artistic creation with his critical, theoretical discourse. Such a reflection is of course infinite and can be exponentiated to ever higher powers and multiplied as "in an endless series of mirrors" (*FS,* 2:182–83; *LF,* 175). Previous types of poetry are "finished and are now capable of being fully analyzed," Schlegel maintained, obviously referring to the classical and classicist kinds of poetry. Modern poetry, however, is in a permanent state of becoming, and he adds that this "in fact, is its real essence: that it should forever be becoming and never be perfected." Modern or romantic poetry "can be exhausted by no theory and only a divinatory criticism would dare try to characterize its ideal" (*FS,* 2:182–83; *LF,* 175).

This infinite becoming, irreducible to a knowable principle with regard to beginning and end, seems to express Schlegel's notion of history most concisely and also best represents the state of an accomplished modernity, fully conscious of its sep-

28. Friedrich Schlegel, *Kritische Ausgabe senier Werke,* ed. Ernst Behler with the collaboration of Jean-Jacques Anstett, Hans Eichner, and other specialists, 35 vols. (Paderborn-München: Schöningh, 1958–). References to this text are designated *FS.* Translations are taken, when available, from Friedrich Schlegel, *Lucinde and the Fragments,* trans. Peter Firchow (Minneapolis: University of Minnesota Press, 1971), and are designated *LF.*

aration from classical perfection and equally distant from any utopian goal of accomplishment. Schlegel illustrated his self-reflective modernism in a great variety of ways, one of which was his frequent use of formulas such as "not yet" or "as long as." Thus, he justifies fragmentary writing "as long as" we have not yet established the completed system of knowledge, or he demands irony "as long as in oral or written dialogues we philosophize not yet fully in systematic fashion" (*FS*, 2:152). In a similar argumentation, philosophy is in need of "genial inspirations" and "products of wit" because it is not yet entirely systematic. This will change, Schlegel assures us, once we move on to a safe methodology (*FS*, 2:200; *LF*, 192). Yet, as we realize at this point, the words "as long as" and "not yet" do not designate a transitoriness to be overcome by accomplished knowledge or a temporary deficiency, but the actual state of our knowledge, its permanent form. Schlegel said: "One can only become a philosopher, not be one. As soon as one believes oneself to be a philosopher, one stops becoming one" (*FS*, 2:173; *LF*, 167).

Yet Schlegel's position can hardly be characterized as sheer scepticism about any achievable goal, since he not only maintains the validity of limited, circumscribed structures of knowledge, but also considers systematic totality and coherence as a necessary, however unattainable goal. In one of his fragments he said: "It is equally fatal for the mind to have a system and to have none. One will simply have to decide to combine the two" (*FS*, 2:173; *LF*, 167). This double obligation of having a system and having none is entirely in line with the fragment quoted earlier about the unending and theoretically inexhaustible course of romantic poetry. On the one hand, no theory, no system will be able to grasp the unpredictable manifoldness of poetry; on the other, a divinatory criticism will always be tempted to characterize its ideal.

Looked at from the standpoint of the quarrel between the ancients and the moderns, this status of modernity certainly indicates a victory of the moderns over the ancients, in that no classical standard any longer determines the course of modern poetry in its future-oriented direction. The price to be paid for this independence, however, is the relegation of pure beauty and perfection to a past age of classical harmony and the ascription of alienation, imperfection, and deficiency to the status of modernity. Modernism in this view appears as a post-classical age in which the classical structures of self-possession and identity are lost. However, the modern age appears as yearning for a lost harmony and mourning a unity that belongs to the past. And in this sense of a mournful grieving for losses and deficiencies, we could still speak of a lingering dominance of the ancients over the moderns or, in more theoretical terms, of a delay in the full manifestation of the modern consciousness or the consciousness of modernity.

Such considerations certainly motivated the feeling of modernity during the romantic age and are typical of the type of humanism that developed in Germany during the age of Goethe. Classical Greece was projected as an image of ideal perfection to which the modern age related in unsatisfied longing. This humanism, like the humanism of the Renaissance, attempted a rebirth of human culture through the sources of classical antiquity. In contrast to the humanism of the Renaissance and European classicism, however, the humanism of the age of Goethe more or less bypassed Roman antiquity and related directly to the Greeks. Greek culture—in poetry, literature, the arts, rhetoric, philosophy, and political life—became a medium for self-recognition and could not simply be shaken off in a modernist posture. A more complex answer with regard to the classical age had to be developed, which finally found expression in the demand for an interaction, a dialectical interrelationship between classicism and romanticism (modernism) as pronounced by Friedrich Schlegel along with his brother.

In this view, classicism and modernism enter into a relationship of close interaction, into a dialectical rapport lacking in the previous treatments of the quarrel between the ancients and the moderns. In paradoxical formulation we could say that the most advanced type of modernity is the one that stands in the liveliest interaction with classical Greece. True modernity does not separate itself from true classicism, but maintains a vivid relationship with the ancient world. Bad modernity, one could say, is a mere separation from classicism, a mere progression. Genuine modernity has an equal relationship to classicism and is in a dynamic competition with that world. One cannot restore the classical age by returning to a past historical time, however perfect that age might have been. Instead, one must produce a timely effort. What the moderns should seek is not the restitution of classical mythology, but the creation of a contemporary, up-to-date "new mythology," not the rejuvenation of the Homeric epic, but the creation of the modern novel as an expression of subjective transcendental poetry.

In this interaction of modernism and classicism, however, the world of the ancients still maintains dominance over the moderns, and Schlegel's construction of modernism, entirely open-ended toward the future ("infinite becoming"), appears to be regulated by the assumption of an absolute classicism. Indeed, he seems to have thought about the Greek world in terms of an unsurpassed exemplariness and maintained in different contexts that Greek poetry was "a general natural history of beauty and art" (*FS*, 23:188, 204), that it contained for all ages "valid and legislative perceptions" (*FS*, 1:318), and that its characteristic was "the most vigorous, pure, distinct, simple, and complete reproduction of general human nature" (*FS*, 1:276). With regard to the theory of poetry, he thought that Greek poetry offered "for all original concepts of taste and art a complete collection of examples all of which were amazingly useful for the theoretical system, as if formative nature had condescended to anticipate the desires of reason in its search for knowledge" (*FS*, 1:307). The formations of this world "do not seem to have been made or generated, but existed eternally or originated by themselves" because they do not call forth "the slightest reminiscence of work, art, and want" (*FS*, 1:298).

Correspondingly, Schlegel speaks about the individual works of Greek poetry in superlatives like "pure beauty," "unpretentious perfection," or "singular majesty" that seems to exist only for itself (*FS*, 1:298). In a more theoretical formulation he describes the character of these works as "perfection" (*FS*, 1:298), as a structured identity with itself in the sense of a complete harmony with itself (*FS*, 1:296). Schlegel was convinced that Greek poetry had reached this "*last limit of natural formation*," this "*highest peak of free beauty*." "*Golden age* is the name for this state," he said and added: "Although this pleasure granted by the works of the golden age of Greek art permits one addition, it is yet without interference and want—*complete and self-sufficient.* I don't know a more appropriate name for this height than '*the highest beauty*'" (*FS*, 1:287). For this image of absolute classicism and perfect exemplariness, he added as a last touch: "*Prototype of art and taste*" (*FS*, 1:288).

The only disturbing element in this characterization of absolute beauty consists in the phrase "although . . . permits one addition." With that phrase, Schlegel's construction of an absolute classicism takes a definite turn toward modernity. For if one follows the meaning of these words, one will soon encounter characteristics of Greek beauty, indeed, all beauty, which in the last analysis render impossible any concept of classicism or a golden age and reduce them to borderline concepts, or ironic metaphors at best. The "addition" Schlegel has in mind in this particular instance reads: "By no means a beauty above which nothing more beautiful can be thought, but the accomplished paradigm of the unattainable idea becoming here fully visible" (*FS*, 1:287–88). He continues: "Art is infinitely perfectible, and an absolute maximum is impossible in its continuous development: but no doubt a contingent, relative maximum exists" (*FS*, 1:287–88). A work of art, in other words, can only be an example "demonstrating the absolute goal of art as visibly as possible in a concrete work of art" (*FS*, 1:293). Among these examples, the works of the golden age of Greek poetry certainly occupy a high rank. They are the "*peak of the natural formation of beautiful art*" and therefore for all ages "*the high prototype for artful progression*" (*FS*, 1:293). This does not alter the fact, however, that these accomplishments are not an absolute goal, not occurring in any time and in any history, but only a maximum of classical formation, that is, a "relative maximum" (*FS*, 1:634).

The classical aesthetics of a complete identity and harmoniously organized structure of the work of art is consequently replaced by a type of artistic creation which exhibits nonidentity, dissimulation, otherness, and difference. In the realm of literature, this results from the medium of poetry, language, as well as from its "organ," the imagination, which renders its products much more "corruptible" as well as "perfectible" than any other art (*FS*, 1:265, 294). This fragile, incomplete character of poetry becomes obvious in its tendency to "cancel the progression and laws of rationally thinking reason, and to transplant us once again into the beautiful confusion of the imagination, into the original chaos of human nature" (*FS*,

2:319). The imagination alone, by no means reason, is capable for Schlegel of embracing the abundance of life in all its perplexing, mysterious, and odd appearances. The imagination, however, is not capable of fully rendering this life of the imagination. The attempt at complete communication is shipwrecked and transforms itself into indirect, ironic communication (*FS*, 2:334), a constant alternation of "self-creation" and "self-destruction" (*FS*, 2:172). The desired poetry becomes a "poetry of poetry" integrating with its creative process the "artistic reflection and beautiful self-mirroring" of the artist and therefore is always and at the same time "poetry and the poetry of poetry" (*FS*, 2:204).

6

Friedrich Schlegel formulated the reflective and self-reflective character of poetry first in the medium of history. Just as there is no final goal for the infinite becoming of poetry and no utopian state where we would land and speak nothing but beautiful language, there is no perfect beginning for poetry in a golden age of pure innocence and naiveté. Classical Greece, if one would like to maintain this image as a model of perfection, is moved from the beginning of European poetry to the unattainable end of history, but even for a "divinatory criticism," it would be impossible "to characterize its ideal" (*IS*, 2:183; *LF*, 175). As Schlegel appeased absolute expectations from the future with formulas like "not yet" or "as long as," we could apply the phrase "always already" with equal effect to our past. We should be careful, however, not to deduce from this view of history any type of indolent indifference, because Schlegel pronounced himself quite strongly against the kinds of historical criticism which he classified as the "postulate of vulgarity" and the "axiom of the average."

He said about these attitudes: "Postulate of vulgarity: everything great, good, and beautiful is improbable because it is extraordinary and, at the very least, suspicious. The axiom of the average: as we and our surroundings are, so must it have been always and everywhere because that, after all, is so very natural" (*FS*, 2:149; *LF*, 145).

Schlegel consequently rejected the Greek myth according to which Orpheus constituted the beginning of Greek poetry. Such an image seemed to imply that poetry had come down from heaven in all its splendor and integrity and only later assumed fragmentation and difference from itself (*FS*, 1: 406–10). For him, the "oldest document" arising out of the night of antiquity was Homeric poetry, but the search into the origin of these poems will get us lost in a retrograding stage-shifting of ever earlier beginnings (*FS*, 1:397). Schlegel also expressed the self-transcending character of poetry in structural terms and characterized romantic poetry because of the close interaction of the poet with his work, as "transcendental poetry," that is, poetry representing "the producer along with its product" (*FS*, 2:204; *LF*, 195). Since total communication is impossible, poetry transforms itself into indirect communication, into saying it otherwise, by spacing and temporalizing. The imagination therefore finds its necessary correspondence in irony, in ironic construction (*FS*, 2:334).

August Wilhelm Schlegel focused on these structural aspects of poetry and related them more directly than any other critic of his time to the nature of language and poetic diction. He liked to chastise art philosophers like Kant, who out of complete ignorance in matters of poetic composition, attributed the poetic effect to some supernatural interference, some "je ne sais quoi," and in their philosophical constructions drew a strong dividing line between genius and taste or between the imagination and reason. Schlegel suggested foregoing the "foreign force" in favor of expanding the notions of genius or imagination by including reason, reflection, critique, and self-criticism among them (*AWS,* 1:14–33).[29] He said: "I fear that this unnameable is nothing but the recognized insufficiency of language to make fully adequate an inner intuition because language only has arbitrary signs which reason attempts to appropriate as much as possible. This illuminates the necessity of not treating the language of poetry solely as an instrument of reason" (*AWS,* 1:16). There was also no original state of poetry from which our poetry had fallen, but poetry, like all of our activities, takes place entirely on this side of the fall (*AWS,* 1:254). Referring to the late eighteenth-century distinction between "natural beauty" and "art beauty" meant to ascertain the derivative character of art in comparison to nature, Schlegel claims that for his romantic theory, art beauty is definitely the "first-born" sister and that one would speak of beauty in nature only once the artistic drive had become active (*AWS,* 1:256–57).

The particular modern thrust in these conceptions of poetry, however, can perhaps best be illustrated through Nietzsche. As a matter of fact, Nietzsche took up some of these notions directly from the Schlegels, especially their discussion of Euripides. The question most directly connected with these topics was that of the beginning of modernism.[30] August Wilhelm Schlegel considered it one of his brother's greatest critical merits in the field of classics to have been the first in the modern age to discern the immeasurable distance sepa-

29. August Wilhelm Schlegel, *Kritische Ausgabe seiner Vorlesungen,* ed. Ernst Behler with the collaboration of Frank Jolles, 6 vols. (Paderborn-Müchen: Schöningh, 1989–). References to this text are designated *AWS.*

30. See Ernst Behler, "A. W. Schlegel and the Nineteenth-Century *Damnatio* of Euripides," in *The Nineteenth-Century Rediscovery of Euripides,* ed. William M. Calder. *Greek-Roman and Byzantine Studies* 27 (1986): 335–67.

rating Euripides from Aeschylus and Sophocles. Friedrich Schlegel thereby revived an attitude the Greeks themselves had assumed toward the poet (*AWS,* 1:747–48). His assessment of Euripides was based on a genetic view of Greek literature in its development from epic to lyric and dramatic poetry, from Homer to Pindar and Sophocles, and during the dramatic age, from harsh greatness (Aeschylus) to high beauty (Sophocles) and luxuriant decay (Euripides). Through A. W. Schlegel's influential writings, this image of Greek literature became dominant throughout the nineteenth century and eventually found its most radical expression in Nietzsche's *The Birth of Tragedy* of 1872. Against this background, Euripides can be viewed in two ways. From the vantage of a stubborn classicism, he can be seen as the detractor of classical tragedy who through innovations such as prologues, the abandonment of the idea of fate, the isolation of the chorus from the action, arbitrariness in the treatment of myth, overabundant usage of the trochaic tetrameter, and so on, had unbalanced the beautiful harmony of the old drama and brought about an "insurrection of the individual parts against the whole" (*AWS,* 1:749). Heine interpreted A. W. Schlegel's critique as that of a classicist pedant who had the habit of "always whipping the back of a younger poet with the laurel-branch of an older one."[31] The other way of viewing Euripides was to say: "In his idea, his genius, and his art, everything else is available in the greatest profusion; only congruity, lawfulness is lacking. With vigor and ease, he knows how to move us, to tease us, to penetrate us into the marrow of the soul, and to excite us through the richest variety. Passion, its rise and fall, especially its vehement outbursts, he portrays incom-

31. Heinrich Heine, *Sämtliche Werke,* ed. Klaus Briegleb (München: Hanser, 1971), vol. 3, 415.

parably" (*FS,* 1:61). This was Friedrich Schlegel's image of Euripides, and here modernity looked into its own face.

Nietzsche shared to a certain degree the pedantic view of a stubborn classicism. In his *The Birth of Tragedy,* Euripides has lost almost all of the "luxuriant" attractions he still displayed in the writings of the Schlegel brothers and appears as a mere decline from the height of classical beauty. To make this decline all the more compelling, Nietzsche advanced the apex of tragic poetry from Sophocles, the model of the Schlegel brothers, to Aeschylus. Nietzsche's critique of aesthetic modernism, as exemplified in Euripides, had thus become much harsher. It was the infusion of reason, of consciousness, reflection, criticism, of philosophy that had destroyed the beauty of the classical tragedy. Euripides was the first dramatist of a "conscious aesthetics" (*FN,* 1:539),[32] and around him there is "a peculiarly broken shimmer, typical of modern artists." His "almost un-Greek aesthetic character" is best summarized by the notion of "Socratism," because Euripides' principle, "Everything has to be conscious to be beautiful," parallels Socrates' statement, "Everything has to be conscious to be good." Nietzsche said, "Euripides is the poet of Socratic rationalism" (*FN,* 1:540). This is perhaps the shortest formula for literary modernism.

And yet, when pressed for the origin of this "aesthetic Socratism" or aesthetic modernism, Nietzsche comes to an answer amazingly close to the Schlegels'. The principles of a "conscious aesthetics" were, first of all, not invented by Socrates or Euripides but resulted from the "historical gap"

32. Friedrich Nietzsche, *Kritische Studienausgabe,* ed. Giorgio Colli and Mazzino Montinari, 15 vols. (Berlin: de Gruyter, 1980). References to this text are designated *FN.* When available, the translation is taken from Friedrich Nietzsche, *The Birth of Tragedy and the Case of Wagner,* trans. Walter Kaufmann (New York: Random House, 1967).

between the Athenian public and classical tragedy (*FN*, 1: 537). Socratism in the sense of a conscious, self-reflective activity, is not only "older than Socrates" but also an element that evolves inherently from art itself and does not need to be implanted from an outside force such as philosophy. It originates with dialectics, dialogue, and language, which were all lacking in the oldest forms of tragedy. Dialogue and dialectics, however, necessarily lead to argument, contest, dispute, and set a process in motion which culminates in the "chess-like" type of drama represented by Euripides (*FN*, 1:546). The symptoms of "decay" are therefore noticeable long before Euripides, already in Sophocles (*FN*, 1:548), maybe in the dialogical form of drama itself, even in chorus and dance. Nietzsche's construction of a division between classicism and modernism takes the same retrograding direction of ever earlier beginnings that was noticeable in the theory of the Schlegel brothers. Properly speaking, we are dealing with processes not really signifiable by historical figures and not representable in historical terms. Euripideism and Socratism appear like immense driving-wheels of a motion that is pre-Socratic as well as post-Socratic and spreads its impact over posterity "like a shadow that keeps growing in the evening sun" (*FN*, 1:97, 635).

3
Irony in the Ancient and the Modern World

Irony is inseparable from the evolution of the modern consciousness. In one respect, irony is a traditional subject, as old as human speech, codified in manuals, defined in its structure, but as unexciting as these scholastic topics are. In another regard, however, irony is virtually identical with that self-reflective style of poetry that became accentuated during the romantic age, and it is a decisive mark of literary modernity. In a move typical of romantic thought, however, irony was then turned around and discovered in works of literature where it had never before been surmised and thus became almost coextensive with literature itself. There is general agreement that this decisive extension of irony to a basic critical term took place toward the end of the eighteenth century and coincided with the formation of the romantic theory of literature. Until then, irony had been understood mostly as a figure of speech, firmly established and registered in rhetoric. We can even specify this turning point much more precisely by referring to a fragment written in 1797 by Friedrich Schlegel and expressing, to all appearances, the new feature of irony for the first time.

The fragment begins with the statement, "Philosophy is the true homeland of irony, which one would like to define as logical beauty" (*FS,* 2:152, no. 42; *LF,* 148)[1]—obviously refer-

1. Friedrich Schlegel, *Kritische Ausgabe seiner Werke,* ed. Ernst Behler with the collaboration of Jean-Jacques Anstett, Hans Eichner, and other specialists, 35 vols. (Paderborn-München: Schöningh, 1958–). References to this

ring to Socratic irony as the first manifestation of the ironic mood in the West. Schlegel goes on to say that there is also a "rhetorical species of irony," which "sparingly used, has an excellent effect, especially in polemics" (*FS,* 2:152, no. 42; *LF,* 148). This phrase of the fragment apparently relates to the dominant usage of irony from Cicero to Swift and Voltaire as a rhetorical device or figure of speech that is good in polemics because it attacks indirectly and not in a vulgar way. Yet compared to the philosophical type of irony, to the "sublime urbanity of the Socratic muse," this rhetorical kind is more pompous. There is one possibility, however, of approaching and equaling the lofty Socratic style of irony, and that is in poetry. For this purpose, however, poetry should not restrict irony to "isolated ironical passages, as rhetoric does," but be ironic throughout, as Socrates was in his dialogues. As a matter of fact, Schlegel continues, there is a poetry that accomplishes precisely this task: "There are ancient and modern poems that are pervaded by the divine breath of irony throughout and informed by a truly transcendental buffoonery. Internally: the mood that surveys everything and rises infinitely above all limitations, even above its own art, virtue, or genius; externally, in its execution: the mimic style of a moderately gifted Italian *buffo*" (*FS,* 2:152, no. 42; *LF,* 148).

In another fragment of the same year, Schlegel describes the ironic mood of Socrates more fully and indicates how such irony should animate poetic works. This irony is an "involun-

---

text are designated *FS.* Translations are taken, when available, from Friedrich Schlegel, *Lucinde and the Fragments,* trans. Peter Firchow (Minneapolis: University of Minnesota Press, 1971). On Schlegel's notion of irony and its historical context see Ernst Behler, "The Theory of Irony in German Romanticism," in *Romantic Irony,* ed. Frederick Garber (Budapest: Kiado, 1988), 43–81. For an interpretation of this topic from the point of view of an intersubjective dialectic of consensus see Gary Handwerk, *Irony and Ethics in Narrative: From Schlegel to Lacan* (New Haven: Yale University Press, 1985).

tary and yet completely deliberate dissimulation" (*FS,* 2:160, no. 108; *LF,* 155) impossible to convey because for one "who hasn't got it, it will remain a riddle even after it is openly confessed." In such an ironic performance, "everything should be playful and serious, guilelessly open and deeply hidden." This irony originates from both naiveté and reflection, nature and art, and is the "conjunction of a perfectly instinctive and perfectly conscious philosophy." The most compact statements about this kind of irony occur in the middle of the fragment and read: "It contains and arouses a feeling of the indissoluble antagonism between the absolute and the relative, between the impossibility and the necessity of complete communication. It is the freest of all licenses, for by its means one transcends oneself; and yet it is the most lawful, for it is absolutely necessary" (*FS,* 2:160, no. 108; *LF,* 156). These few quotes already indicate the close link between the new notion of irony and the consciousness of literary modernity that marked the beginning of romanticism.

1

When Schlegel decided to term the mood which permeates certain works by Boccaccio, Cervantes, Sterne, and Goethe ironic, he caused indeed a fundamental change in Western critical thought. The authors just mentioned would have been somewhat astonished to hear him interpret their literary creations as displaying irony—to say nothing of Shakespeare and other older models of the ironic style. For until Schlegel, irony had retained its classical meaning as a figure of speech, and the only reason why we today do not find anything remarkable in Schlegel's formulations is that his usage of the term took root and became established. Until then, far into the eighteenth century, the word irony had kept its strict and consistent connotation of an established form of speech or communication which could be reduced to the simple formula: "a figure of speech by which one wants to convey the opposite of what one says."[2] This is a quote from the French *Encyclopedia* of 1765 and contains the essence of the definitions of irony found in numerous handbooks of various European literatures as they had developed from older manuals of rhetoric concerning the art of public speaking and persuasion.

If in the schematized structure of classical rhetoric we were to seek the place for irony, we would find it first in the column of the tropes, that is, among indirect modes of speech (including metaphor, allegory, metalepsis, and hyperbaton); and second under the rubric of figures of speech, that is, of particular verbal constructions (including question, anticipation, hesitation, consultation, apostrophe, illustration, feigned regret, and intimation). The most basic characteristic of all forms of classical irony is always that the intention of the speaker is opposed to what he actually says, that we understand the contrary of what he expresses in his speech. We should perhaps add to this description that according to ancient opinion, in order to distinguish irony from mere lying, the entire tenor of speaking, including intonation, emphasis, and gesture, was supposed to help reveal the real or intended meaning. Irony is mostly discussed by the classical rhetoricians in the context of peculiar idiosyncrasies of style. Aristotle mentions irony in the third book of his *Rhetoric,* which is devoted to style, and presents it as a "mockery of oneself": "Some of the forms befit a gentleman, and some do not; irony befits him more than does buffoonery. The jests of the iron-

2. *Encyclopédie ou dictionnaire raisonné des Sciences, des Arts et des Métiers, par une Société de Gens de Lettres* (Geneva: Pellet, 1777), vol. 19, 86.

ical man are at his own expense; the buffoon excites laughter at others."[3] From other passages of his works, especially his *Ethics,* we know that Aristotle conceived of irony as a noble self-deprecation. "Irony is the contrary of boastful exaggeration," he said; "it is a self-deprecating concealment of one's powers and possessions—it shows better taste to deprecate than to exaggerate one's virtues."[4]

Cicero, who introduced the term into the Latin world and rendered it as "dissimulation" ("ea dissimulatio, quam Graeci *eirōneia* vocant"),[5] discussed irony in his work *On the Orator* in connection with figures of speech. He defined irony as saying one thing and meaning another, explaining that it had a very great influence on the minds of the audience and was extremely entertaining if it was presented in a conversational rather than declamatory tone.[6] Finally, Quintilian assigned irony its position among the tropes and figures discussed in the eighth and ninth books of his *Oratorical Education*, where its basic characteristic is that the intention of the speaker differs from what he actually says, that we understand the contrary of what he expresses in speech ("in utroque enim contrarium ei quod dicitur intelligendum est").[7] In addition to these two formal modes of irony, however, Quintilian mentions a third which transcends the scope of mere rhetoric, or what Schlegel would call single ironic instances, and relates to the whole manner of existence of a person. Quintilian refers directly to Socrates, whose entire life had an ironic coloring

3. Aristotle *Rhet.* 3.18.1419b7. English translation by Lane Cooper (New York: Appleton, 1932), 240. Aristotle is quoted from *Aristotelis Opera: Edidit Academia Borussica* (reprint, Darmstadt: Wissenschaftliche Buchgesellschaft, 1960).

4. Aristotle *Eth. Nic.* 2.7.1108a19–23, 4.13.1127a20–26.

5. Cicero *Acad. Pr.* 2.5.15.

6. Cicero *De or.* 2.67.270.

7. Quintilian *Inst. or.* 9.2.44.

because he assumed the role of an ignorant human being lost in wonder at the wisdom of others.[8]

As this observation indicates, Quintilian, as well as Cicero and other rhetoricians, regarded Socrates as the master of irony, the *eirōn*. Originally, however, the words *eirōneia* and *eirōn* had a low and vulgar connotation, even to the extent of being an invective. We come across these terms in Aristophanes' comedies, in which the ironist is placed among liars, shysters, pettifoggers, hypocrites, and charlatans—in other words, with deceivers.[9] Plato was the first to present Socrates as an ironic interlocutor who by understating his talents in his famous pose of ignorance, embarrassed his partner and simultaneously led him into the proper train of thought. With the Platonic Socrates, the attitude of the ironist was freed from the burlesque coarseness of classical comedy and appeared with that refined, human, and humorous self-deprecation that made Socrates the paragon of the teacher.

Yet even in Plato's dialogues, where the attitude of Socratic irony is so obviously present, the term irony itself still retains its derogatory cast in the sense of hoax and hypocrisy and as such, evinces the Sophist attitude of intellectual deception and false pretension. In his *Republic,* for example, Plato depicts the scene in which Socrates deliberates, in characteristic fashion, on the concept of *dikaiosunē,* that is, justice. At a crucial point in the discussion, his conversational partner Thrasymachus explodes, requesting Socrates to desist from his eternal questioning and refuting and finally to come out with a direct statement and reveal his own opinion. Again assuming his stance of ignorance, Socrates replies that it is utterly difficult to discover justice and they should have pity

8. Quintilian *Inst. or.* 9.2.46.
9. Aristophanes *Nubes* 443.

rather than scorn for him. At this point, Thrasymachus bursts out: "By Heracles! Here again is the well-known dissimulation of Socrates! I have told these others beforehand that you would not answer, but take refuge in dissimulation." The Greek term rendered here by dissimulation is of course *eirōneia,* irony (337a).[10]

From many other instances in Plato's dialogues we know that the pretended ignorance of Socrates was considered by many of his contemporaries as chicanery, scorn, or deceptive escapism, all of which made him deserve the epithet *eirōn.* Only through Aristotle did the word irony assume that refined and urbane tinge marking the character of "Socratic irony." This significant change in meaning can be detected in Aristotle's *Nicomachian Ethics,* where *eirōneia* and *alazoneia,* understatement and boastfulness, are discussed as modes of deviation from truth. Aristotle, however, held the opinion that irony deviates from truth not for the sake of one's own advantage, but out of a dislike for bombast and to spare others from feelings of inferiority. Irony was therefore a fine and noble form. The prototype of this genuine irony was to be found in Socrates, and with this reference irony received its classical expression.[11] Some of the other few instances in which Aristotle mentions irony also reveal a Socratic image. In his *Physiognomy,* Aristotle describes the ironist as possessing greater age and having wrinkles around his eyes reflecting a critical power of judgment.[12] In his *History of Animals,* Aris-

10. Plato is quoted from the edition *Platon: Oeuvres complètes,* ed. Guillaume Budé (reprint, Paris: Les Belles Lettres, 1953). References to this edition are given with the counting according to Stephanus, a counting used in most editions of Plato.

11. Aristotle *Eth. Nic.* 4.13.127b22–26.

12. Aristotle *Phys.* 3.808a27.

totle considers eyebrows rising upward toward the temples as marks of the mocker and ironist.[13]

These physiognomical features which predestined Socrates as the master of irony can also be discovered in Plato's writings about the philosopher. This aspect of Socrates comes forth in the *Symposium* in the speech delivered in Socrates' honor by Alcibiades when he compares Socrates with the Sileni, those carved figurines with satyrlike and grotesque images on the exterior, but pure gold inside. This is obviously a reference to the contrast between the philosopher's outer appearance, his protruding lips, paunch, and stub nose, and his personal rank and intellectual quality. This contrast can also be seen as a form of ironic dissimulation, as a "mask," and has become a famous and continuous theme in European literature. Toward his fellow citizens, Socrates assumes the mask of one who tends to appreciate handsome young men and convivial symposia, who is to all appearances universally ignorant and unfit for any practical activity. But once beneath the surface, we discover that he is above the attractions of physical beauty as well as those of wealth and popular esteem, and that he possesses an unparalleled degree of self-control. Using the Greek term *eirōneia* for this type of dissimulation, Alcibiades explains to his drinking companions: "He spends his whole life pretending and playing with people, and I doubt whether anyone has ever seen the treasures which are revealed when he grows serious and exposes what he keeps inside" (216d).

2

Schlegel obviously had all these different elements in mind when in 1797 he portrayed Socratic irony, intending to utilize

13. Aristotle *Hist. Animal.* 1.491b17.

this model for an understanding of literature and poetry. At that time he was deeply impressed by Goethe's novel *Wilhelm Meister,* which had just been completed (1796) and became famous through Schlegel's review for the "irony hovering above the entire work" (*FS,* 2:137). In one of his notebooks Schlegel wrote: "Meister = ironic poetry as Socrates = ironic philosophy because it is the poetry of poetry" (*FS,* 18:24, no. 75), that is, self-conscious and self-reflective poetry. He was also aware that Socratic irony had been extinguished in the classicist tradition of the *ars poetica* by a glossy and formal device of rhetorical irony that followed established rules and, in its firm strictures of truth-oriented relations, constituted almost the opposite of what Socratic irony once had been. Although in rhetorical irony the intention of the speaker is contrary to what he actually says, rules insure that we actually understand the intended meaning. This irony is based on complete agreement, perfect understanding between speaker and listener, and an absolute notion of truth.

A good illustration of the transition from the classical concept of rhetorical irony to that type of romantic irony which Schlegel had in mind can be found in Thomas Mann's *The Magic Mountain.* Thomas Mann was an authority on matters of irony, not only through his literary practice, but also in theory, and liked to blend historical-critical disquisitions with his fiction. The following piece, part of one of the endless discussions between the Italian Settembrini and the engineer Hans Castorp in a Swiss sanatorium, is a good example of this technique. It begins when the Italian retorts to a remark by Castorp:

> "Oh heavens, irony! Guard yourself, Engineer, from the sort of irony that thrives up here: Guard yourself altogether from taking on this mental attitude! Where irony is not a direct and classical device of oratory, not for a moment equivocal to a

> healthy mind, it makes for depravity, it becomes a drawback to civilization, an unclean traffic with the forces of reaction, a vice. As the atmosphere in which we live is obviously very favorable to such miasmic growth, I may hope, or rather, I must fear, that you understand my meaning."[14]

Schlegel's position can be exactly characterized as replacing that "direct and classical device of oratory not for a moment equivocal to a healthy mind" with a different type of irony characterized in Mann's text in ironic fashion as "slovenly, anarchic, and vicious." In one respect, this is the most modern type of irony coinciding with a heretofore nonexistent style of literary modernity. Yet in another regard, this is the oldest type of irony in the West, deriving from Socrates and Platonic dialogues.

In varying formulations, Schlegel attempted to rescue the Socratic-Platonic irony of a configurative, indeterminable, self-transcending process of thinking and writing and to integrate it with the modern style of self-reflection and self-consciousness as the decisive mark of literary modernity. In his late lectures about *Philosophy of Language and Word* (1829), he characterized irony as the "astonishment of the thinking mind about itself which often dissolves into a gentle smile" and "beneath a cheerful surface" incorporates "a deeply hidden sense, another higher meaning, and often the most sublime seriousness" (*FS*, 10:353). In Plato's presentation of this thoroughly dramatic development of thought, Schlegel saw the dialogue form as so essentially dominant "that even if we eliminated the titles and names of persons, all addresses and responses, and the entire dialogue format as well, and stressed only the inner thread of thoughts in their cohesion

14. Thomas Mann, *The Magic Mountain,* trans. H. T. Lowe-Porter (New York: Vintage, 1969), 220.

and progression—the whole would still remain a dialogue in which each answer calls forth a new question and which in the alternating flow of speech and counter-speech, or rather of thought and counter-thought, moves forth in lively fashion" (*FS*, 10:35).

The "alternating flow of speech and counter-speech, or rather of thought and counter-thought," seems to constitute an essential aspect in Schlegel's view of an ironic configuration of thought or writing. We should be careful, however, not to construe this movement in dialectical or Hegelian manner as a goal-oriented, teleological process, but to consider instead a bottomless sliding as its main feature. Again referring to Plato's manner of writing, Schlegel in his *Lessing's Thoughts and Opinions* (1804) described this character of modern prose with the image of an infinite trajectory:

> A denial of some current prejudice or whatever else can effectively surmount innate lethargy constitutes the beginning; thereupon the thread of thought moves imperceptibly forward in constant interconnection until the surprised spectator, after that thread abruptly breaks off or dissolves in itself, suddenly finds himself confronted with a goal he had not at all expected: before him an unlimited wide view, but upon looking back at the path he has traversed and the spiral of conversation distinctly before him, he realizes that this was only a fragment of an infinite cycle. (*FS*, 3:50)

Schlegel's most famous formulations for the alternating flow of speech and counter-speech or thought and counter-thought are his manifold paraphrases of a constant alternation of affirmation and negation, of exuberant emergence from oneself and self-critical retreat into oneself, of enthusiasm and scepticism in fragments from before the turn of the century. These phrases are all but different formulations for his theory of "poetic reflection" and "transcendental poetry," which coincides with his notion of irony often rendered as a "constant alternation of self-creation and self-destruction" (*FS* 2:172, no. 51; *LF*, 167). A similar and recurrent formulation of the same phenomenon is the phrase "to the point of irony," or "to the point of continuously fluctuating between self-creation and self-destruction" (*FS* 2:172, no. 51; 217, no. 305; *LF*, 167, 205). This is the point of the highest perfection for Schlegel, that is, of a perfection which is conscious of its own imperfection by inscribing this feature into its own text. Another and perhaps better way of formulating the counter-movement of self-creation and self-destruction inherent in the status of "to the point of irony" would be to say that this is by no means a deficiency but rather the highest level we can reach, and in an aesthetic consideration, also one of charm and grace.

In his early writings on Greek poetry, Schlegel represented the counter-movement of self-creation and self-destruction as a self-inflicting movement against a primordial Dionysian ecstasy and said, "The most intense passion is eager to wound itself, if only to act and to discharge its excessive power" (*FS* 1:403). One of his favorite examples for such action was the *parabasis* of classical comedy, that is, the sometimes capricious, frivolous addresses of the poet through the chorus and the coryphaeus to the audience that constituted a total disruption of the play. In a fragment from 1797, Schlegel says summarily, "Irony is a permanent *parabasis*" (*FS* 18:85, no. 668),[15] taking the emergence of the author from his work in the broadest sense and relating it to ancient and modern literature in all its genres. With specific reference to the comic exuberance exhibited through *parabasis* in the comedies by Aristophanes, Schlegel said: "This self-infliction is not ineptitude, but deliberate impetousness, overflowing vitality, and often has not

15. Schlegel uses the less usual term "parekbasis."

a bad effect, indeed stimulates the effect, since it cannot totally destroy the illusion. The most intense agility of life must act, even destroy; if it does not find an external object, it reacts against a beloved one, against itself, against its own creation. This agility then injures in order to excite, not to destroy" (*FS* 1:30). In the medium of modern literature, Schlegel described the ironic mood in Goethe's *Wilhelm Meister* by referring to the author's "air of dignity and self-possession, smiling at itself," or to the occurrence of the most prosaic scenes in the middle of the poetic mood, and adds, "One should not let oneself be fooled when the poet treats persons and events in an easy and lofty mood, when he mentions his hero almost never without irony, and when he seems to smile down from the heights of his spirit upon his master work, as if this were not for him the most solemn seriousness" (*FS* 2:133).

3

Within the field of philosophy, Schlegel's irony attempts to bring to our attention the "inexhaustible plenitude and manifoldness of the highest subjects of knowledge" (*FS* 13:207) and to unmask the "idol of the highly praised omniscience" (*FS* 13:208). With this critique, however, Schlegel provoked that contemporary philosopher who like no one else before claimed to have access to "absolute knowledge" and indeed considered irony the greatest challenge to his own position—Hegel. In an extremely sharp polemic, certainly constituting one of the main intellectual events of the romantic age, Hegel singled out Friedrich Schlegel as the "father of irony" and the "most prominent ironic personality" (*GWFH* 11:233)[16] in the

16. Georg Wilhelm Friedrich Hegel, *Werke in 20 Bänden* (Frankfurt: Suhr-

modern age and chastised irony as annihilating scepticism, as irresponsible arbitrariness, as the apex of isolated subjectivity separating itself from the unifying substance (*GWFH* 7:278).[17] In his lectures on *Aesthetics,* Hegel criticized the artistic aspects of that irony "invented by Herr Friedrich von Schlegel" as a "divine ingenuity for which everything and anything is nothing but an insignificant creation, unrelated to the free creator, who feels himself rid of his products once and for all because he can just as well create as annihilate them" (*GWFH* 13:95).

Of particular importance in this regard is Hegel's critique of irony, ironic consciousness, and Schegel's theory in his *Phenomenology of Spirit* of 1807. To be sure, Schlegel's name does not occur once in this text, but in a now famous investigation of 1924, Emanuel Hirsch established that the concluding passage of the part on morality dealing with conscience is an encoded critique of philosophers contemporary with Hegel.[18] The section on the "moral view of the world" (*GWFH* 3:464–94)[19] refers to Kant, whereas the following sections take on the representatives of the romantic generation one by one: "moral ingenuity" related to Jacobi, "absolute certainty of oneself" to Fichte, the "beautiful soul" to Novalis, "dissemblance" to Schleiermacher, the "heart of stone" to Hölderlin, and the "avowed evil" to Friedrich Schlegel. In the figure of

---

kamp Taschenbuch Wissenschaft, 1986). References to this text are designated *GWFH.*

17. This expression is not a literal quote from Hegel, who usually says "apex of subjectivity recognizing itself as the ultimate" (*GWFH* 7:278), but a compilation by Otto Pöggeler which very well expresses the line of thought in Hegel's philosophy of law. See Otto Pöggeler, *Hegels Kritik der Romantik* (Bonn: Bouvier, 1956), 66.

18. Emanuel Hirsch, "Die Beisetzung der Romantiker in Hegels Phänomenologie," in *Materialien zu Hegels Phänomenologie des Geistes,* ed. Hans Friedrich Fulda and Dieter Henrich (Frankfurt: Suhrkamp, 1979), 245–75.

19. *Hegel's Phenomenology of Spirit,* trans. A. V. Miller (Oxford: Oxford University Press, 1977), 365–74.

"forgiveness," however, Hegel depicted his own position reconciling the split of consciousness into "beautiful soul" and "dissemblance." Taken together, all of these figures manifest a progression, an enhancement of self-consciousness, one after the other. The culmination of this process is that "reconciling yes" which unites all particular forms of certainty and is "God manifested in the midst of those who know themselves in the form of pure knowledge" (*GWFH* 3:494).

If the position of the avowed evil actually represents Friedrich Schlegel, this strange hierarchy expresses an extremely high regard for irony. All previous forms of consciousness are not yet fully conscious of themselves. They are diffuse manifestations, based on illusions, and lacking the last mental awareness of themselves. The form of evil consciousness, however, has the function of driving conscience to its last consequence by avowing evil in the statement "It is I" (*GWFH* 3:490). For Hegel, this is "the highest revolt of the mind conscious of itself." According to the Hegelian principles of dialectic, however, this highest form of negativity precisely motivates the "activity of the idea" and is thereby essential for the reconciling yes (*GWFH* 3:492). Yet seen in itself, the evil stage of consciousness is the purest negativity, the spirit that always negates, the apex of isolated subjectivity separating itself from the unifying substance.

Although such encoded texts always maintain a certain indeterminateness as far as historical points of reference are concerned, Hegel's other writings, especially his *Philosophy of Law,* make it sufficiently obvious that he had Schlegel in mind when he depicted the position of "absolute evil" in the *Phenomenology of Spirit.* For these texts relate such assumptions directly to irony and Schlegel (*GWFH* 7:279–80). They make these references, however, no longer in apocalyptic images but in direct polemics and are often not free from strong animosity and outbursts of hatred (*GWFH* 18:461). In Hegel's *Philosophy of Law,* for instance, Schlegel's irony is "not only the evil, that is, the entirely general evil in itself, but also adds the form of evil, subjectivity, vanity, by proclaiming to know itself as the vanity of all content, and to know itself in this knowledge as the absolute" (*GWFH* 7:279). As a participant in Hegel's Berlin lectures, Kierkegaard observed that "on every occasion" Hegel seized the opportunity to speak up against irony and scolded Schlegel and his disciples as "incorrigible and stubborn sinners." Kierkegaard said: "Hegel always discussed them in the most disparaging manner; indeed Hegel looks down with intense scorn and disdain at these 'superior persons,' as he often calls them. . . . But the fact that Hegel has become infuriated with the form of irony nearest to his own position has naturally distorted his concept of the concept. And if the reader seldom gets a discussion, Schlegel, on the other hand, always gets a drubbing" (*CI,* 282).[20]

The proximity of Schlegel's irony to Hegel's own position noticed by Kierkegaard seems to relate to Hegelian dialectic, which also appears to be animated by a constant yes and no, a permanent construction and suspension, an alternation of self-creation and self-destruction, an inherent "negativity." Some of the most recent interpretations of Hegel today indeed tend to link Hegel very closely with the romantic theory of Friedrich Schlegel,[21] although Schlegel's irony certainly

20. Søren Kierkegaard, *The Concept of Irony with Constant Reference to Socrates,* trans. Lee M. Capel (New York: Harper and Row, 1965). References to this text are designated *CI.*

21. Otto Pöggeler, "Grenzen der Brauchbarkeit des deutschen Romantik-Begriffs," in *Romantik in Deutschland,* ed. Richard Brinkmann (Stuttgart: Metzler, 1978), 341–54; Otto Pöggeler, "Ist Hegel Schlegel?" in *Frankfurt aber ist der Nabel dieser Erde,* ed. Christoph Jamme and Otto Pöggeler (Stuttgart: Klett-Cotta, 1982), 325–48; Rüdiger Bubner, "Zur dialektischen Bedeutung

lacks the teleology and goal-oriented drive of Hegel's dialectical thought process. The entire structure of Hegelian thought appears to be oriented toward some kind of landing or arriving in a completed philosophy, a system, providing the ground for the perfected philosophy of law and the perfected human society, the State, the unifying substance. To keep the opposite tendencies of Schlegel and Hegel apart, one should characterize this as a relationship of two fundamentally contradictory types of knowledge that cannot be reduced to a common ground and therefore form a complete and unresolvable opposition. The Hegelian type of knowledge claims a total intellectual comprehension of the interpretation of the finite and the infinite. Schlegel insists that this relationship can never be reduced to a structure or a dialectic comprehensible by finite knowledge, but constitutes an infinite process graspable only in aspects. To relate these discourses of the early nineteenth century more to our manner of thinking, we could also say that in Hegel and Schlegel respectively, we encounter models of thought, forms of knowledge, and modes of philosophical certitude that correspond to the entirely different discourses of structuralism and poststructuralism of hermeneutics and deconstruction in our time.

Yet even if we insist on a fundamental difference between Hegel and Schlegel, we come across irony in the center of Hegel's own philosophy. In his lectures on *The History of Philosophy,* Hegel, as usual, engages in enraged diatribes against irony, negating this attitude as mere play with everything, which dissolves all higher and divine truth into nothingness, into ordinariness, and so on (*GWFH* 18:460–61). At this

---

romantischer Ironie," in *Die Aktualität der Frühromantik,* ed. Ernst Behler and Jochen Hörisch (Paderborn: Schöningh, 1987), 85–95.

point, however, all of a sudden, Hegel draws a parallel between irony and dialectics by saying in one single parenthesis, "All dialectic respects everything that should be respected as if it were respected, lets the inner destruction generate on it—universal irony of the world" (*GWFH* 18:460). Heine and Kierkegaard, who attended Hegel's lectures, took notice of this remarkable incident. Kierkegaard tried to explain this irony using the world-historical individual, the tragic hero of world history. Such a hero has to bring about a new level of historical reality by displacing the old order, but is bound to an actuality that will equally become subject to change (*CI*, 276–77). Kierkegaard thought that Hegel had quite correctly described this "universal irony of the world": "Inasmuch as each particular historical actuality is but a moment in the actualization of the Idea, it bears within itself the seeds of its own destruction" (*CI*, 279). Indeed, Hegel himself had made the tragic fate of the "world-historical individualities" a central theme of his lectures on the *Philosophy of History* (*GWFH* 12:45–50).

Yet more precisely speaking, it is not so much the dialectical and world historical destruction of noble individualities as such which creates irony, but rather the eye, the observation, the consciousness of the one who views this destruction as a necessary concomitant and precondition of world historical development and of life in general. It is first of all the philosopher's, Hegel's, consciousness that is ironic because he observes the dialectical evolution of world history which moves on through contradictions and out of necessity destroys forms of life, so that other, higher forms can emerge. Hegel sensed irony in this dialectical consideration according to which existing historical forms appear as both firmly respected and yet at the same time subject to necessary destruction. In a second consideration, however, Hegel was, of course, convinced that this entire process was governed by reason and meaning and that the world spirit moved on, despite all destruction, "exalted and glorified" (*GWFH* 12:98). This consciousness of a higher meaningfulness increased the irony on the part of the philosopher in a certain way, especially since the agents on the world historical stage did not share this overall view and quite often appeared duped by a higher destiny.

What about irony, however, if the conviction of an overriding meaningfulness is fading? The first to anticipate this problem was perhaps Benjamin Constant, who in 1790 toyed with the idea "that God, i.e., the author of us and our surroundings, died before having finished his work . . . that everything now finds itself made for a goal which no longer exists, and that we especially feel destined for something of which we ourselves have not the slightest idea."[22] Constant advanced this speculation in a letter which was not published until the beginning of our century and could hardly have occasioned the rise of topics such as world-historical irony, God's irony, and universal irony of the world as they now developed on an anti-Hegelian foundation and from the position of God's death. It was Heine who articulated these themes in a deliberately ironic context. In his *The Book* LE GRAND of 1826, for instance, he describes the world as the

> dream of an intoxicated God who has stolen away surreptitiously from the carousing assembly of the Gods and lain down to sleep on a lonely star and does not know himself that he also creates everything he dreams, and dream images take shape, often madly lurid, but harmoniously sensible—the *Iliad,* Plato, the battle of Marathon, Moses, the Medicean Venus, the Strass-

22. Gustave Rudler, *La jeunesse de Benjamin Constant* (Paris: Colin, 1909), 377.

> burg cathedral, the French Revolution, Hegel, steamships, etc. are excellent individual ideas in this creative divine dream. Yet it won't be long before the God will awaken and rub his sleepy eyes and smile!—and our world will have vanished into nothing, indeed, will have never existed. (*SW* 2:253)[23]

It is in this context that Heine uses terms such as "God's irony" and the "irony of the world," and refers to the "irony of the great poet of the world stage up there." He calls God the "Aristophanes of heaven," the "author of the universe," who has "admixed to all scenes of horror in this life a good dose of merriment," or he is of the opinion that "Our good Lord is still yet a better ironist than Mr. Tieck" (*SW* 2:424, 522, 282; 3:427). Contrary to Hegel, Heine's notion of "God's irony" and "irony of the world" results from the disappearance of the conviction of reasonable order in this world and derives from that "great rupture through the world" which has "torn asunder the world, right through the middle," but also goes right through the center of the heart of the poet, which, like the "center of the world," has been "badly torn asunder" (*SW* 3:304). "Once the world was whole," Heine says, "in antiquity and the Middle Ages, and in spite of all apparent fights there was still a unity of the world, and there were whole poets. We will honor these poets and derive delight from them; yet every imitation of their wholeness is a lie—a lie discovered by every sane eye and then necessarily subject to disdain" (*SW* 3:304).

4

It was Nietzsche, however, who drew the most radical consequences from these discussions of a universal irony of the world. In one instance he even referred to the term with its

23. Heinrich Heine, *Sämtliche Werke,* ed. Klaus Briegleb (Munich: Hanser, 1971). References to this text are designated *SW*.

Hegelian flavor, when he attempted to describe his own attitude in entirely classical terms, but then inadvertently added a decidedly modern ingredient to it, saying: "*amor fati* [love of my fate] is my innermost nature. But this does not preclude my love of irony, even world-historical irony" (*FN* 6:363; *GM*, 324).[24] Yet Nietzsche usually avoided the term irony, which for his taste had too much romanticism in it, and preferred the classical notion of dissimulation which he translated as "mask." In his unpublished fragments, for instance, Nietzsche regarded the "increases in dissimulation" as indices of an ascending order of rank among beings: "In the organic world, dissimulation appears to be lacking; in the organic, cunning begins; plants are already masters in that. The highest human beings like Caesar, Napoleon (Stendhal's word about him), [are] the same as the higher races (Italians), the Greeks (Odysseus) [in this regard]; slyness belongs to the *essence* in the elevation of the human being" (*FN* 8:10, 159).

In the few instances where we come across the term in Nietzsche's writings, irony has mostly a negative connotation. The early text *On the Uses and Disadvantages of History for Life* (1874), for instance, depicts irony as the attitude of "practical

24. Friedrich Nietzsche, *Kritische Studienausgabe,* ed. Giorgio Colli and Mazzino Montinari, 15 vols. (Berlin: de Gruyter, 1980). References to this edition are designated *FN*. When possible, the following translations were utilized: Friedrich Nietzsche, *The Birth of Tragedy and the Case of Wagner,* trans. Walter Kaufmann (New York, Random House, 1967); Friedrich Nietzsche, *Untimely Meditations,* trans. R. J. Hollingdale (Cambridge: Cambridge University Press, 1986); Friedrich Nietzsche, *Daybreak,* trans. R. J. Hollingdale (Cambridge: Cambridge University Press, 1982); Friedrich Nietzsche, *The Gay Science,* trans. Walter Kaufmann (New York: Random House, 1974); Friedrich Nietzsche, *Beyond Good and Evil,* trans. Walter Kaufmann (New York: Random House, 1966); Friedrich Nietzsche, *On the Genealogy of Morals: Ecce Homo,* trans. Walter Kaufmann and R. J. Hollingdale (New York: Random House, 1969); Friedrich Nietzsche, *Twilight of the Idols: The Anti-Christ,* trans. R. J. Hollingdale (New York: Penguin Books, 1968).

pessimists," of historical scholarship in the sense of déjà vu, without any regard for the future. The "ironic existence" and the "type of *ironic self-awareness*" that come to light here have "indeed a kind of inborn gray-hairedness" and manifest themselves in "senile occupations," those of "looking back, of reckoning up, of closing accounts, of seeking consolation through remembering what has been, in short, historical culture" (*FN* 1:303; *UM*, 101). Combined with such a retrospective attitude was the premonition that the future had little in store in which one could really rejoice, and thus people lived on with the feeling: "If only the ground will go on bearing *us!* And if it ceases to bear us, that too is very well." Nietzsche adds, "that is their feeling and thus they live an *ironic* existence" (*FN* 1:302; *UM*, 100). He admits that everything human requires the "ironic consideration" as far as its "genesis" is concerned, but this is precisely the reason why irony is so superfluous in the world for him (*FN* 2:210; *HH*, 120). Habituation to irony spoils the character according to Nietzsche: "in the end one comes to resemble a snapping dog which has learned how to laugh but forgotten how to bite" (*FN* 2:260; *HH*, 146–47).

Historically speaking, the origin of irony was the "age of Socrates," that is, a life "among men of fatigued instincts, among the conservatives of ancient Athens who let themselves go—'toward happiness,' as they said; toward pleasure, as they acted—and who all the while still mouthed the ancient pompous words to which their lives no longer gave them any right." In this world, irony was needed, Nietzsche said: "*irony* may have been required for greatness of soul, that Socratic sarcastic assurance of the old physician and plebeian who cut ruthlessly into his own flesh, as he did into the flesh and heart of the 'noble,' with a look that said clearly enough: 'Don't dissemble in front of me! Here—we are equal'" (*FN* 5:146; *GE*,

138). Irony was also operative in the modern age as a necessity for existence. Nietzsche found it in the "morality of mediocrity," a morality that spoke of "measure and dignity and duty and neighbor love" while pursuing only the continuation and propagation of its own type. Such a morality, he thought, "will find it difficult *to conceal its irony*" (*FN* 5:217; *GE,* 212).

Altogether, irony appeared to Nietzsche as one of the many forms of life that represented decadence. Irony was the shoulder-shrugging on the part of the scholar "who sees nothing in philosophy but a series of *refuted* systems and a prodigal effort that 'does nobody any good'" (*FN* 5:130; *GE,* 122). Irony is that "Jesuitism of mediocrity which instinctively works at the annihilation of the uncommon man and tries to break every bent bow or, preferably, to unbend it" (*FN* 5:134; *GE,* 126). The ironist is a "person who no longer curses and scolds," who no longer knows how to affirm and to negate (*FN* 5:135; *GE,* 126). Yes and no go against his taste. Instead, he likes to maintain a "noble abstinence" by repeating "Montaigne's 'What do I know?' or Socrates' 'I know that I know nothing!' Or: 'here I don't trust myself, here no door is open to me!' Or: 'Even if one were open, why enter right away?' Or: 'What use are all rash hypotheses? Entertaining no hypotheses at all might well be part of good taste. Must you insist on immediately straightening what is crooked? on filling up every hole with oakum? Isn't there time? Doesn't time have time? O you devilish brood, are you incapable of *waiting?* The uncertain has its charms, too; the sphinx, too, is a Circe; Circe, too, was a philosopher'" (*FN* 5:137–38; *GE,* 129–30).

As always when Nietzsche touches upon subjects of decadence, however, his straightforward evaluations begin to shift and soon let us notice his predilection for such phenomena. The last quote cited was taken from his aphorism on scepticism. This aphorism moves on to describe contemporary

France, which for Nietzsche "now really shows its cultural superiority over Europe by being the school and display of all charms of scepticism." In similar fashion, France has always possessed "a masterly skill at converting even the most calamitous turns of its spirit into something attractive and seductive" (*FN* 5:139; *GE,* 130–31). Decadence now appears in a favorable light. The aphorism, in turn, is only one of a whole series inspired by Baudelaire, French romanticism, and symbolism, all closely related to Nietzsche's treatment of irony.[25] For that investigation, however, we have to transcend the restrictions set by the word irony.

One good access point to the complex configuration of irony in Nietzsche's writings, often presented as an art of living, an *ars vitae,* a *savoir vivre,* is the theme of the mask as he unfolded it in the sections "The Free Spirit" and "What Is Noble?" from *Beyond Good and Evil.* That this topic relates to the classical notions of *dissimulatio* and *eirōneia* is indicated by the impression that the most prominent aphorism on the mask, no. 40 of *Beyond Good and Evil,* seems to pick up the Socratic image of the Silenus, although the name of Socrates does not occur in the text. Nietzsche says in this aphorism: "I could imagine that a human being who had to guard something precious and vulnerable might roll through life, rude and round as an old green wine cask with heavy hoops: the refinement of his shame would want it that way" (*FN* 5:58; *GE,* 51). This contrast is one of the main points in the discussion—as are shame, avoidance of openness, and nakedness—and stimulates the question of

25. See on this Karl Pestalozzi, "Nietzsches Baudelaire-Rezeption," in *Nietzsche-Studien* 7 (1978): 158–78; and Mazzino Montinari, "Nietzsches Auseinandersetzung mit der französischen Literatur des 19. Jahrhunderts," in *Nietzsche heute: Die Rezeption seines Werkes nach 1968,* Amherster Kolloquium 15, ed. Sigrid Bauschinger, Susan L. Cocalis, and Sara Lennox (Bern: Franke, 1988), 137–48.

whether "nothing less than the opposite" might be the "proper disguise for the shame of a god" (*FN* 5:57; *GE,* 50). With regard to human actions, Nietzsche continues: "There are occurrences of such a delicate nature that one does well to cover them up with some rudeness to conceal them; there are actions of love and extravagant generosity after which nothing is more advisable than to take a stick and give any eyewitness a sound thrashing: that would muddle his memory. Some know how to muddle and abuse their own memory in order to have their revenge at least against this only witness: shame is inventive" (*FN* 5:57–58; *GE,* 50–51).

Toward the end of the aphorism Nietzsche concentrates on the communicative actions of such a "concealed" human being who "instinctively needs speech for silence and for burial in silence." Such a person is "inexhaustible in his evasion of communication" and obviously "*wants* and sees to it that a mask of him roams in his place through the hearts and heads of his friends." Here we realize that the original reference points of semblance and truth, appearance and reality, concealment and shame are lost and cannot be reconstituted. Indeed, Nietzsche continues with regard to the desire for a mask on the part of the human being: "And supposing he did not want it, he would still realize some day that in spite of that a mask of him is there—and that is well. Every profound spirit needs a mask: even more, around every profound spirit a mask is growing continually, owing to the constantly false, namely *shallow,* interpretation of every word, every step, every sign of life he gives" (*FN* 5:58; *GE,* 51).

Another form of masking and "one of the most refined disguises" is Epicureanism or "a certain ostentatious courage of taste which takes suffering casually and resists everything sad and profound" (*FN* 5:225–26; *GE,* 220–21). Other people "employ cheerfulness because they are misunderstood on its account—they *want* to be misunderstood" (*FN* 5:226; *GE,* 220). Science is another disguise which creates "a cheerful appearance," and those who employ science do so "because being scientific suggests that a human being is superficial—they *want* to seduce others to this false inference" (*FN* 5:226; *GE,* 220–21). Free and insolent minds want to conceal that they are broken hearts (Hamlet, Galiani), and sometimes "even foolishness is the mask for an unblessed all-too-certain knowledge." From all this follows for Nietzsche that it is "a characteristic of more refined humanity to respect 'the mask' and not to indulge in psychology and curiosity in the wrong place" (*FN* 5:226; *GE,* 221).

As a "hermit," Nietzsche also did not believe that any philosopher "ever expressed his real and ultimate opinions in books" and indeed doubted "whether a philosopher could *possibly* have 'ultimate and real' opinions" (*FN* 5:234; *GE,* 229). Perhaps such a philosopher writes books precisely to conceal what he harbors, so that one wonders "whether behind every one of his caves there is not, must not be, another deeper cave—a more comprehensive, stranger, richer world beyond the surface, an abysmally deep ground behind every ground, under every attempt to furnish 'grounds'" (*FN* 5:234; *GE,* 229). The conclusion to which we are driven by such considerations appears to be: "Every philosophy also *conceals* a philosophy; every opinion is also a hide-out, every word also a mask" (*FN* 5:234). Yet here again, it belongs to the marks of a refined style of humanity and philosophizing to respect the mask of the philosopher and not to indulge in skeptical thoughts such as: "There is something arbitrary in his stopping *here* to look back and to look around, in his not digging deeper here but laying his spade aside; there is also something suspicious about it" (*FN* 5:234; *GE,* 229).

Such a will to truth at any price belongs to a youthful state of philosophizing which assaults "men and things in this manner with Yes and No." This is the "worst of tastes, the taste for the unconditional," and one needs to be cruelly fooled and abused by this taste before one learns the "art of nuances," puts "a little art into one's feelings," and "risks trying even what is artificial—as the real artists of life do" (*FN* 5:49; *GE,* 43). "No," Nietzsche says in his preface to *The Gay Science,* "this bad taste, this will to truth, to truth 'at any price,' this youthful madness in the love of truth, have lost their charm for us: for that we are too experienced, too serious, too merry, too burned, too *profound.* We no longer believe that truth remains truth when the veils are withdrawn; we have lived too much to believe this. Today we consider it a matter of decency not to wish to see everything naked, or to be present at everything, or to understand and 'know' everything" (*FN* 3:352; *GE,* 38).

We could go on to show the relevance of the mask to Nietzsche's own existence, his life as a double, a *Doppelgänger* (*FN* 6:266; *GM,* 225), or to style: "long, difficult, hard, dangerous thoughts and the *tempo* of the gallop and the very best, most capricious humor" (*FN* 5:47; *GE,* 40–41). However, it already seems sufficiently evident that ironic dissimulation, configurative thinking and writing, double-edged communication, and artistry of living and philosophizing were his response to the universal irony of the world. Nietzsche took up this topic when, in *The Gay Science,* he raised the question of "what would happen if everything upon which our ultimate convictions rest would become incredible, if nothing should prove to be divine any more unless it were error, blindness, the lie—if God himself should prove to be our most enduring lie?" (*FN* 3:577; *GS,* 283).

From this vantage point, Nietzsche was not certain whether "wanting not to allow oneself to be deceived" was really "less harmful, less dangerous, less calamitous" than allowing oneself to be deceived, "whether the greater advantage is on the side of the unconditionally mistrustful or the unconditionally trusting" (*FN* 3:575–76; *GS*, 280–81). His answer to this dilemma was the admonition: "Let us be on our guard!" as he developed it in an aphorism with the same title. This aphorism takes its point of departure from the realization that the "total character of the world, however, is in all eternity chaos—in the sense not of a lack of necessity but of a lack of order, arrangement, form, beauty, wisdom, and whatever other names there are for our aesthetic anthropomorphisms" (*FN* 3:468; *GS*, 168). To assume a "world of truth" that is supposed to have "its equivalent and its measure in human thought and human valuations" and could be "mastered completely and forever with the aid of our square little reason" was for Nietzsche "crudity and naiveté, assuming that it is not mental illness, an idiocy" (*FN* 3:625; *GS*, 335). Such a world is "not a fact, but an imaginative fabrication and elaboration on a sum of meager observations; such a world is 'in flux' as something becoming, but as an ever alternating falsity which will never approximate truth: because—there is no 'truth'" (*FN* 12:114). To assume, however, that Nietzsche had reduced this "whole marvelous uncertainty and rich ambiguity of existence" (*FN* 3:373; *GS*, 76) to a monistic principle such as the will to power or to the complementary interrelationship of will to power and eternal recurrence would certainly fall short of his rich deployment of the universal irony of the world.

5

It is indeed a widely shared opinion, even among his enemies, that Nietzsche was the "turntable" for the postmodern period, moving around the course and direction of modern intellectual history. The main evidence for this view is his radicalized critique of reason, truth, morality, religion, and all the ordering principles on which Western thought relied. This crucial position can just as well be attributed to Nietzsche's manner of writing, his ironic affiliation of truth and illusion, mask and authenticity, life and decadence. Several modern authors borrowed their irony directly from Nietzsche and admitted this frankly. We have only to think of André Gide, Thomas Mann, and Robert Musil. Thomas Mann openly declared that the event which Nietzsche constituted in his life bears the single name of "irony."[26] In spite of the close proximity to Nietzsche among the writers who would consider themselves as candidates for postmodernism, however, they lack such a clear alliance with irony. This reluctance about irony and avoidance of the word could already be noticed in Nietzsche and in his case certainly had something to do with the anti-romantic campaign he believed himself to be conducting. In postmodernist writing, however, the shunning of irony seems to be related to the prominent position of irony in the modern intellectual world, its concomitant relationship to reason, and its mitigating function amidst a general rationalism. Irony seems to have compromised itself through this alliance and therefore appears unfit for describing the postmodern mood, although there is perhaps no better word for this complex phenomenon.

Paul de Man seems to be the only exception to this attitude. He described his theory of literature clearly in terms of irony and came to a position which equated irony with any type of text. De Man never considered himself a postmodern critic,

26. Thomas Mann, *Reflections of a Nonpolitical Man,* trans. Walter D. Morris (New York: Ungar, 1983), 13.

however, but this can perhaps be attributed to the fact that this term was not yet in vogue at the time of his writing or simply explained by the observation that hardly any writer would apply this term to himself. Yet the entire structure of de Man's thought, especially his convictions about the figurative character of language and the resulting polysemy of meaning in every human expression, perfectly qualifies him for such a status, not to speak of the application of his ideas by his students, whose techniques of "undoing a reading" or "letting the text fall back upon itself" have become stereotypes of postmodern criticism.

One reason for the prominence of irony in de Man's writings may simply have been the new criticism. Just as irony had been the "principle of structure" in literary works for some of the new critics (e.g., Cleanth Brooks), irony was for de Man the principle of disrupture in a literary text. Whereas the new criticism saw irony, ambiguity, and paradox as forging together the multiplicity and variety of a poetic work to an organic whole of integrality, harmony, complete identity with itself, and self-presence, de Man conceived of irony in terms of a discrepancy between sign and meaning, a lack of coherence among the parts of a work, a self-destructive ability on the part of literature to articulate its own fictionality, and an inability to escape from a situation that has become unbearable. Irony practically coincides with his notion of deconstruction, his interpretative techniques according to the mottos of *Blindness and Insight* and *Allegories of Reading*.

De Man also delved into the historical evolution of irony as a characteristic of modern consciousness from Friedrich Schlegel to Kierkegaard and Nietzsche with its French correspondence in Baudelaire's *On the Essence of Laughter*. Already in the essay on "The Rhetoric of Temporality" (1969), de Man comes close to his later version of "radical irony" ("you can't be a 'little bit ironic'")[27] when he describes the "absolute irony" which, in his opinion, all these authors have approached in terms of a consciousness of madness, a consciousness of non-consciousness, the end of consciousness.[28] This irony is no longer a trope, not even "the trope of tropes," but the innermost essence of literature for de Man: a rupture, an interruption, a disruption of language which makes it impossible for the author to master his text and for the reader to register unambiguous reading protocols. The problems with this concept of irony are that it brings us back to the classrooms of literary criticism and rhetoric and that it is exclusively preoccupied with the gloomy sides of writing in the sense of restriction, inhibition, and incapability. De Man's irony practically coincides with every linguistic articulation and is, so to speak, an involuntary by-product of language. For Schlegel too, irony was involuntary, yet at the same time absolutely deliberate and conscious (*FS* 2:160; *LF*, 155). In de Man's conception, irony loses all ambiguity in the sense of deliberate structuring on the part of the author and in this dull generality even appears to be diffused.

The heart of the problem is certainly that it is practically impossible to write about post-Nietzschean irony without being too narrow, or without openly contradicting oneself if one attempts to move beyond the limits of a simple yes or no. As in the case of Nietzsche, this type of irony is best conveyed in action, through performance, a kind of writing which in the mood of a joyful wisdom employs the logic of play and the rules of a game. This is perhaps best accomplished in the

27. Robert Moynihan, "Interview with Paul de Man: Introduction by J. Hillis Miller," *Yale Review* 73 (1983–84): 579.

28. Paul de Man, "The Rhetoric of Temporality," in *Blindness and Insight*, 2d ed. (Minneapolis: University of Minnesota Press, 1983), 216.

writings of Jacques Derrida. His texts, from this formal point of view, appear as a congenial contemporary correspondence to the tradition of irony in the modern period. Derrida too avoids the word irony, at least he does not accord any prominence to it in his writings. The closest we get to his concept of irony is perhaps in his discussion of the "dissimulation of the woven texture" at the beginning of *Plato's Pharmacy.* "A text is not a text," Derrida says in that instance, "unless it hides from the first comer, from the first glance, the law of its composition and the rules of its game. A text remains, moreover, forever imperceptible. Its laws and rules are not, however, harbored in the inaccessibility of a secret; it is simply that they can never be booked, in the present, into anything that could rigorously be called a perception."[29] The text among Derrida's writings, however, that could be considered the most direct continuation of the discourse of irony in the style of our time and that unfolds a structure similar to that of universal irony in previous discussions, is his essay on *Différance* of 1968.[30]

In contrast to Schlegel's and Hegel's dialectical style of affirmation and negation and Nietzsche's vitalistic antagonism of life and decadence, this text is cast in the medium of structuralism, of formal, differential, semiological functioning, and the concept of difference is directly derived from that formal tradition. By combining this discourse with the metaphysical or antimetaphysical discourses of Nietzsche, Freud, and Heidegger, Derrida gives the semiological discussion of

29. Jacques Derrida, *Plato's Pharmacy,* in *Dissemination,* trans. Barbara Johnson (Chicago: The University of Chicago Press, 1981), 63.

30. Jacques Derrida, "Différance," in *Speech and Phenomena and Other Essays on Husserl's Theory of Signs,* trans. David B. Allison and Newton Garver (Evanston: Northwestern University Press, 1973), 129–60. References to this text are designated *D.*

"difference" new momentum. Taken in this broad sense, however, Derrida's notion of difference seems to suggest a philosophical counterposition to the metaphysics of presence and identity as it has dominated Western thought since its origin. Yet such an approach would fundamentally misconstrue difference and differential thinking from the outset as an alternative to presence, as a mere upsetting of the previous system, or simply as an opposition to it. Such a relationship of difference to presence and identity would finally remain within the realm of the system and only create a new identity and presence in reverse of the former. The task is rather to exhibit difference not as an opponent but as an inhabitant of any structure of identity, not as the atomization but as the functioning of structure, not as a deprivation or suspension of meaning but as the mode of existence of meaning. A similar model of thought can be seen in the principle of negativity inherently operative in Hegelian dialectic or in Schlegel's irony. To appreciate fully the functioning of all such operations, one has to leave behind the negative connotations that our language unavoidably attributes to phenomena such as negativity and difference in relationship to presence and identity, as well as any chronological or teleological type of relationship in the sense of prior and posterior among them.

Derrida's thinking about difference is directly inspired by Saussure's theory of language. Language, in Saussure's conception, is a system of signs in which the relationship of the signs to what they signify—for example, of words to things, of sounds to ideas—is not natural, "ontic," or in any other way unavoidable, but "arbitrary." The signs of language, in other words, are not autonomous entities in themselves, but elements of a system, and they are not positively determined through their content, but negatively through their differences from other elements of the system. They are that which the others are not. Language, in this regard, is not a system of identities, but one of differences. This principle of a determination through differences became the decisive aspect of formal and differential functioning in semiotics and the guiding principle of modern structuralism. For Derrida, however, these modern attempts to think of the mere "structurality of structure" as a structure simply in its function and without anything outside of it did not fully accomplish their goal and eventually took recourse to an extrastructural ground on which one centered the display of differences.[31] Saussure, for instance, gave the expressive substance, the human voice, a privileged position, and Lévi-Strauss assigned archaic and natural societies a special status. In a more general way, we can see the entire course of occidental metaphysics as successive performances of centering structures and take the various names given to these centers as chapters in the history of metaphysics: the world of ideas, God, transcendental consciousness, and so on (*SSP,* 279–80). Derrida's own attempt could indeed be described, at least partly, as an avoidance of such grounding or as thinking of structure purely as a function, an operation, a display of difference in an infinite exchange of signs or in an unrestricted economy.

The notion of difference seems to point in this direction, and deconstructive enterprises such as the decentering of structures, the upsetting of taxonomies, or the reversal of meaning and signification appear to exemplify this intention. Yet Derrida's inspirations are by no means only structuralist ones and have aside from "spacing" and "temporalizing" a

31. See on this Jacques Derrida, "Structure, Sign, and Play in the Discourse of the Human Sciences," in *Writing and Difference,* trans. Alan Bass (Chicago: The University of Chicago Press, 1978), 278–94. References to this text are designated *SSP.*

number of distancing and dissociating techniques differentiating his attempt from the conception of a closed, controllable, systematized, or "structured" set of signs. To emphasize this multiple thinking of difference, Derrida mentions right at the beginning of his essay on *Différance* and several times during the course of the text that difference is a theme in which the "most characteristic feature of our 'epoch'" (*D*, 135–36) can be thought out, in which we can see "the juncture—rather than the summation—of what has been most decisively inscribed in the thought of what is conveniently called our 'epoch'" (*D*, 130). He also says that our "epoch" can be characterized "as the delimitation of ontology (of presence)" (*D*, 153). As instances of this thinking in terms of difference, Derrida cites besides "Saussure's principle of semiological difference": the "difference of forces in Nietzsche," the "possibility of facilitation [frayage, Bahnung], impression and delayed effect in Freud," the "irreducibility of the trace of the other in Levinas," and the "ontic-ontological difference in Heidegger" (*D*, 153). These names and topics indicate that the transgression of the occidental metaphysics of presence is not only at work in the new linguistics and semiotics of structuralism, but in the historical, philosophical, and psychoanalytical discourses of our time as well and that this transgression, this overcoming of the constrictions of the tradition, might very well be considered the mark of our epoch.

In his essay on Lévi-Strauss of about the same time (1966), Derrida laid out a similar image of the tendency of the epoch as a moving away from a centering ground, the unifying and ordering principle of traditional metaphysics. If we asked when this decentering occurred, Derrida argues in that text, it would be somewhat naive to refer to a particular "event," a doctrine, or an author as the most visible mark of this break, because this occurrence is no doubt part of the totality of an era, perhaps our own, but has "always already" proclaimed itself and begun to work. Nevertheless, if we still insisted on choosing a few names, just as an indication, and recalled "those authors in whose discourse this occurrence has kept most closely to its most radical formulation," we doubtlessly would come to the following three names. We would cite Nietzsche's "critique of metaphysics, the critique of the concepts of Being and truth, for which were substituted the concepts of play, interpretation, and sign (sign without present truth)." Second, we would have to cite Freud's "critique of self-presence, that is, the critique of consciousness, of the subject, of self-identity and of self-proximity or self-possession." And third, we would cite Heidegger's "destruction of metaphysics, of onto-theology, of the determination of Being as presence" (*SSP*, 280).

Derrida's notion of a surpassing of metaphysics, however, requires the same cautionary attitude as his structuralist concept of difference in relationship to presence and identity and is in the last analysis only another expression of the same phenomenon, but in historical formulation. This surpassing or transformation of metaphysics rests on subtle distinctions of closure and end. What is comprised in the transgression of a closure—end of metaphysics, end of philosophy, end of man—can endure indefinitely. The transgression in the sense of closure does not land or arrive in a beyond of metaphysics, but in the grasp of metaphysics can go on endlessly, just as with regard to the beginning of this movement, we have noticed that it has "always already" proclaimed itself and begun to work.

Yet beyond the structuralist model of difference in relation to identity and the historical image of a transgression of the metaphysics of presence, there is still a third way of tracing out difference, which relates to the semantic aspects of signifying differential functions in language, in philosophical discourse, and in writing. Strictly speaking, we are moving here into a zone which our language actually does not permit us to articulate. Almost all of the words and concepts used to describe difference, and especially such terms as interval, dividing, retention, and protention, rest on the metaphysics of identity and self-presence which Derrida attempts to dislocate, to decenter, and to deconstruct. Difference thereby appears to be the most stringent example of the "impossibility and necessity of complete communication" which Schlegel listed among the characteristics of irony. This linguistic indisposition, if we call it provisionally by this negative name, is for Derrida only another sign of difference. Language, looked at from this perspective, is not derived from a speaking subject and is not a determinable function of this subject, but this subject is inscribed in language, is a function of language, conforms to the deployment of difference, and is part of the game.

Derrida is fully conscious that he is caught up in a circle as far as the task of designating difference is concerned and that he will never be able to transcend the thinking of presence and identity because his language will not permit him to do that. Yet he considers it as absurd to renounce the concepts of metaphysics if one is engaged in shaking metaphysics. "We have no language—no syntax and no lexicon—which is foreign to this history," Derrida says: "we can pronounce not a single deconstructive proposition which has not already had to slip into the form, the logic, and the implicit postulations of precisely what it seeks to contest." We could not even pronounce the word "sign" without maintaining our complicity with metaphysics because sign always means "sign of" and thereby reestablishes the metaphysics of presence it wants to upset. These concepts are by no means isolated elements or independent atoms but integrated with a syntax and a system. Borrowing one of them conjures up the entirety of metaphysics (*SSP*, 280–81). This is the position of a bind, a double bind, requiring a double play, a double gesticulation. And it is with these techniques that Derrida's writings accomplish a continuation and reformulation of irony in the modern discourse.

4
Irony and Self-Referentiality

In general, and independent of any specification according to historical time, the most crucial issues of irony reside in the area of self-conscious saying and writing and concern the problems of linguistic articulation, communication, and understanding in regard to truth. The ironic manner of expression can be described as attempting to transcend the restrictions of normal discourse and straightforward speech by making the ineffable articulate, at least indirectly, through a great number of verbal strategies, and accomplishing what lies beyond the reach of direct communication. This attitude, however, automatically constitutes an offense to common reason and understanding—an offense not necessarily intended by the ironist but somehow involuntarily connected with his claim and almost regularly taken as such by the public. Socrates was the first example for that constellation.

The implicit critique of reason and rationality in ironic communication likewise provoked very severe criticism in the modern age. Hegel not only criticized irony as vanity and destructiveness, but even mobilized the apocalypse to depict this attitude as the final incarnation of evil, the beast from the abyss. The opposition to Nietzsche is operative not so much in critical and polemical works written against his philosophy as in decisive reductions of his thought, in eliminating the rich ambiguities and infinite reflection from his text, in leveling out his multiple style to that of a habitual philosopher, the "last metaphysician," who professed square doctrines such as the will to power as the ultimate result of his thinking. In the case of Derrida, the reaction is not so much manifest in a practice-oriented Marxist type of critique as in the hermeneutic indignation about the loss of continuity, agreement across borders, and unambiguous consent among discussion partners which is replaced by a discontinuous, fragmentary, and ironic mode of communication.

The particular reproach in which this critique is phrased is that of a performative self-referential contradiction necessarily implied in any totalized critique of reason and philosophy: one cannot criticize reason and philosophy in an absolute manner without pulling away the basis from underneath this critique, without disavowing this critique, which is itself an expression of reason and rationality. As one easily realizes, this reproach is directed not only against the deconstructive manner of criticizing reason and metaphysics but against the entire sceptical-ironical discourse of modernity as well. Characteristically enough, the ironic discourse itself, because of its highly self-reflective character, practices critical, deprecating observations of a self-referential nature as a constantly recurring technique. It has a particular predilection for toying with antinomies and self-contradictions imposed upon us by our being inscribed in language, by the subterranean determination imposed upon us through language. A self-critical awareness of our linguistic embeddedness has indeed been a characteristic mark of modernity since the romantic age and reached a new intensity with Nietzsche.[1] The three authors chosen as representatives of this discourse, Schlegel, Nietzsche, and Derrida, thematize the self-referential implications of their irony in their own text and through such reflections

1. See on this Constantin Behler, "Humboldt's 'radikale Reflexion über die Sprache' im Lichte der Foucaultschen Diskursanalyse," in *Deutsche Vierteljahresschrift* 63 (1989), 1–24; Josef Simon, "Grammatik und Wahrheit," *Nietzsche-Studien* 1 (1972): 1–27.

accomplish that which Schlegel circumscribed as the "irony of irony" (*FS* 2:369).[2] After having deduced, with all possible rigor, the will to power as the ultimate reality, Nietzsche asks mockingly, "Supposing that this is only an interpretation—and you will be eager enough to make this objection?—well, so much the better" (*FN* 5:37; *GE,* 30–31).[3] Derrida's reflections on an involuntary complicity of deconstruction with metaphysics have to be seen from a similar perspective.

1

Turning to difference and Derrida's essay on *Différance*[4] more specifically, we should first of all notice that the verb *to differ* has two distinct meanings in French (différer) as well as in Latin (differre)—to differ and to defer—and can therefore

2. Friedrich Schlegel, *Kritische Ausgabe seiner Werke,* ed. Ernst Behler with the collaboration of Jean-Jacques Anstett, Hans Eichner, and other specialists, 35 vols. (Paderborn-München: Schöningh, 1958–). References to this edition are designated *FS.* Translations are taken, when available, from Friedrich Schlegel, *Lucinde and the Fragments,* trans. Peter Firchow (Minneapolis: University of Minnesota Press, 1971), designated *FS.*

3. Friedrich Nietzsche, *Kritische Studienausgabe,* ed. Giorgio Colli and Mazzino Montinari, 15 vols. (Berlin: de Gruyter, 1980). References to this edition are designated *FN.* When possible, the following translations were utilized: Friedrich Nietzsche, *The Birth of Tragedy and the Case of Wagner,* trans. Walter Kaufmann (New York, Random House, 1967); Friedrich Nietzsche, *Untimely Meditations,* trans. R. J. Hollingdale (Cambridge: Cambridge University Press, 1986); Friedrich Nietzsche, *Daybreak,* trans. R. J. Hollingdale (Cambridge: Cambridge University Press, 1982); Friedrich Nietzsche, *The Gay Science,* trans. Walter Kaufmann (New York: Random House, 1974); Friedrich Nietzsche, *Beyond Good and Evil,* trans. Walter Kaufmann (New York: Random House, 1966); Friedrich Nietzsche, *On the Genealogy of Morals: Ecce Homo,* trans. Walter Kaufmann and R. J. Hollingdale (New York: Random House, 1969); Friedrich Nietzsche, *Twilight of the Idols: The Anti-Christ,* trans. R. J. Hollingdale (New York: Penguin Books, 1968).

4. Jacques Derrida, "Différance," in Jacques Derrida, *Speech and Phenomena and Other Essays on Husserl's Theory of Signs,* trans. David B. Allison and Newton Garver (Evanston: Northwestern University Press, 1973), 129–60. References to this text are designated *D.*

indicate difference in two basically distinct connotations: "On the one hand, it indicates difference as distinction, inequality, or discernibility; on the other, it expresses the interposition of delay, the interval of a *spacing* and *temporalizing* that puts off until 'later' what is presently denied, the possible that is presently impossible" (*D*, 129). Using the letter *a* from the present participle of "différante," Derrida builds a noun with a visible, yet inaudible spelling error, "*différance*," that is supposed to refer to differing in both senses "as spacing/temporalizing and as a movement that structures every dissociation," that is, to difference as postponement and to difference as distinction (*D*, 129–30, 136–37). The *a* in the title and the following usage of the monstrous word is therefore no printing error, but a deliberate infusion by Derrida to make difference differ more from itself than it normally does (*D*, 129).

Such a creation, however, is "neither a word nor a concept" (*D*, 130). Attempting to sketch out the nature of différance and its multiple structure, we discover that its essence "cannot be exposed," since we can expose only that which at a certain moment can be represented as present, as "the truth of a present or the presence of a present" (*D*, 134). Différance, however, has "neither existence nor essence" and cannot even be defined in the sense of negative theology, indeed it is "irreducible to every ontological or theological—onto-theological—reappropriation" and instead "opens up the very space in which onto-theology—philosophy—produces its system and history" (*D*, 134–35). Given the a-logical structure of différance, the phenomenon also does not permit any order of discourse, of procedure, in developing its content in a reasonable sequence and no longer allows "the line of logico-philosophical speech," not even that of "logico-empirical speech." What remains beyond these alternatives of a regular philosophical approach, however, is the activity of play, and one way of outlining the potentialities of différance is indeed through insisting on the semiotic dimensions in the notion of play.

In classical semiotics the playful character in the functioning of signs is extinguished by the "authority of presence." Signs are mere substitutes for things and thereby of a secondary and provisional character. The sign is secondary, since it is "second after an original and lost presence," and provisional "with respect to its final and missing presence" (*D*, 138). On the basis of Saussure's new linguistics, however, Derrida can say: "Every concept is necessarily and essentially inscribed in a chain or a system, within which it refers to another and to other concepts, by the systematic play of differences" (*D*, 140). Différance, in this regard, is the play of differences, the "movement of play." The effects in this play or the productions of it are not the result of a "subject or substance, a thing in general, or a being that is somewhere present and itself escapes the play of difference." They are rather "traces" that cannot be taken out of their context, cannot be isolated from the interplay of différance (*D*, 141).

When these effects appear "on the stage of presence," they are always related to something other than themselves. Such an effect, such a trace "retains the mark of a past element and already lets itself be hollowed out by the mark of its relation to a future element" (*D*, 142). Its presence is therefore constituted in relation "to what it is not, to what it absolutely is not" (*D*, 142–43). In order to take full cognizance of the interplay of differences at work here, we should not misconstrue past and future as a "modified present" nor overlook the "interval" separating the present from the past as well as from the future. This interval also divides "the present in itself" and divides "along with the present, everything that can be conceived on its basis, that is, every being—in particular, for our metaphysical language, the substance or subject" (*D,* 143). In brief, the present has to be seen, in the perspective of différance, "as a 'primordial' and irreducibly nonsimple, and therefore in the strict sense, nonprimordial synthesis of traces, retentions, and protensions" (*D,* 143). Différance in no case can be derived "from a being-present, one capable of being something, a force, a state, or power in the world, to which we could give all kinds of names: a *what,* or being present as a *subject,* a *who*" (*D,* 145).

We thus come to a notion of différance without origin, without *archē* (*D,* 145–46). At an earlier point, we had realized that according to the requirements of différance, the relationship of originality and derivation cannot be assumed between the subject and its language, that language is not a function of the speaking subject, and that the subject is rather inscribed in language. This elimination of origin, of *archē* has to be maintained with regard to everything in semiology and down to every concept of sign "that retains any metaphysical presuppositions incompatible with the theme of différance" (*D,* 146).

Yet the question remains whether the subject, before it enters the sphere of differences through speaking and signifying, does not enjoy a presence and self-presence "in a silent and intuitive consciousness" (*D,* 146). Consciousness, prior to speech and signs, then would grant us "self-presence, a self-perception of presence," the status of a "living present" (*D,* 147). "This privilege," Derrida says, "is the ether of metaphysics, the very element of our thought insofar as it is caught up in the language of metaphysics." In our century, however, it was Husserl who, with the project of transcendental phenomenology, focused on this topic most directly and investigated the structures of pure consciousness most rigorously. In order to deconstruct this position, one would have to show that presence and specifically consciousness ("the being-next-to-itself of consciousness") are definitely not the "absolutely matrical form of being" but a "determination," an "effect," that is, an effect within a system "which is no longer that of presence but that of différance." Derrida adds to the formulation of this task that the system of presence is so tight that merely to designate this proposal "is to continue to operate according to the vocabulary of that very thing to be de-limited" (*D,* 147).

Here one should notice, however, that Derrida himself attempted to carry out this task in an early investigation particularly devoted to Husserl, transcendental phenomenology, and pure consciousness.[5] The main point in Derrida's own critique of Husserl is that the basic principle of transcendental phenomenology, that is, spaceless and timeless self-representation of meaning in a "living present," is shipwrecked because of the figurative character of language, the "stream of consciousness" and "inner time," and all the relationships to a non-present implied in these experiences: that of a non-identity inscribed into the present as well as that of death written into life. We should add, however, that the conception of a transcendental consciousness independent of language, time, and the "life world" had become highly problematical for Husserl himself. Indeed, one major thrust in Derrida's critique of Husserl is to point out discrepancies between the old metaphysical dream of pure self-presence and the actual results obtained through Husserl's phenomenological investigations.

At this point in mapping out différance, Derrida leaves the semiological discourse and turns to Nietzsche and Freud who "questioned the self-assured attitude of consciousness" and in their own ways came to the conception of différance in regard to consciousness through completely different types of philo-

5. *La voix et le phénomène* of 1967. See the translation listed in footnote 4, above.

sophical argumentation (*D*, 148). Nietzsche accomplished this turn through his "active interpretation" of the "evasions and ruses of anything disguised," his replacement of "truth as a presentation of the thing itself in its presence" by "an incessant deciphering" (*D*, 149). The result of Nietzsche's interminable deciphering or infinite interpretation is "a cipher without truth, or at least a system of ciphers that is not dominated by truth values" (*D*, 149). Différance, in the case of Nietzsche, is the "'active' (in movement) discord of the different forces and of the differences between forces which Nietzsche opposes to the entire system of metaphysical grammar, wherever that system controls culture, philosophy, and science" (*D*, 149).

With Freud, the questioning of the primacy of presence as consciousness assumes the particular twist of a "questioning of the authority of consciousness." The two different meanings of difference embodied in différance, difference as distinction and as delay, are "tied together in Freudian theory" as is obvious in Freud's concepts of trace, facilitation, breaching, memory, inscription, uncensored talking, and deferring (*D*, 149–50). Derrida concentrates on the particular notion of detour (*Aufschub*) as Freud developed it in his *Beyond the Pleasure Principle* and according to which the ego's instinct of self-preservation motivates a momentary replacement of the pleasure principle by the reality principle. "This latter principle," Freud argues, "does not abandon the intention of ultimately obtaining pleasure, but it nevertheless demands and carries into effect the postponement of satisfaction, the abandonment of a number of possibilities of gaining satisfaction and the temporary toleration of unpleasure as a step on the long indirect road (*Aufschub*) to pleasure" (*D*, 150).[6] We can of course

6. Sigmund Freud, "Jenseits des Lustprinzips," in *Sigmund Freud, Studienausgabe* (Frankfurt: Fischer Taschenbuch, 1982). vol. 3, 219–20.

also see the model of delay, of postponement, in the movement of life protecting itself through the deferment of death, or in the activity of memory, even in the operation of culture, and come to similar manifestations of différance in a Freudian context on the basis of Freud's structural model of the psyche.

Yet under no circumstances should we interpret Freud's economic movement of différance in the sense of Hegelian dialectics according to which the deferred presence will always be recovered, and which "amounts to an investment that only temporarily and without any loss delays the presentation of presence" (*D*, 151). Hegel's system is one of a "restricted economy" that has "nothing to do with an unrestricted expenditure, with death, with being exposed to nonsense," whereas the unreserved thinking of différance in the style of Freud is a "game where whoever loses wins and where one wins and loses at the same time" (*D*, 151). Freud's unconscious is not "a hidden, virtual, and potential self-presence," not "a mandating subject" that sits somewhere, not "a simple dialectical complication of the present," but "radical alterity," that is, "a 'past' that has never been nor will ever be present" and "where 'future' will never be produced or reproduced in the form of presence" (*D*, 152).

2

What is questioned through these various modes of thinking différance for Derrida is the "determination of being in presence, or in beingness" (*D*, 153)—beingness in the sense of a determinable principle, an ascertainable ground of all beings. This questioning almost immediately leads to the consideration of whether "différance finds its place within the spread of the ontic-ontological difference" as it was conceived in the "Heideggerian meditation" (*D*, 153) and proposed by this philosopher as ontological difference, as the difference between

Being and beings. As Heidegger had maintained since the appearance of *Being and Time* (1927), the distinction between *Being,* as the ground of all beings, and the variety of *beings* had been the most general and universal presupposition of occidental metaphysics, yet was never questioned in its assumptions. All the metaphysical edifices of Western thought had been built on this foundation, but it was so shaky, according to Heidegger, that all buildings resting on it appeared to be brittle. The most questionable aspect of this ontological difference between Being and beings for Heidegger was that the notion of Being resulting from this difference necessarily remains so vague and abstract that only the most general things can be predicated about Being (*HN* 4:157).[7] Being, in other words, instead of being thought, became excluded from our thinking and was involved in a process of oblivion and forgottenness of such boundless nature "that the very forgottenness is sucked into its own vortex" (*HN* 4:193).

This is for Heidegger the most crucial event in the Occident, in the face of which he expressed his bewilderment throughout his long writing career in an ever-varying fashion: "In the history of Western thought, from its inception, the Being of beings has indeed been thought, but the truth of Being as Being remains unthought; not only is such truth denied as possible experience for thinking, but Western thought, as metaphysics, expressly though unwittingly conceals the occurrence of this refusal" (*HN* 3:189–90). If we did not conceal this refusal, we would have to admit that the foundations on which we continue to build one form of metaphysics after another "*are no foundation at all*" (*HN* 4:163).

7. Martin Heidegger, *Nietzsche,* trans. David Farrell Krell and others, 4 vols. (San Francisco: Harper and Row, 1979–85). References to this text are designated *HN.*

Closely connected with this emphasis on the "ontological difference" in Western thought is for Heidegger the task of a critical removal of all the compounds of thought resulting from it. This project is first outlined in *Being and Time* with the title of a "phenomenological destruction of the history of ontology," a destruction of metaphysics.[8] In this attempt, Heidegger's project is directly related to Derrida's deconstruction of metaphysics. In both cases, the critique of metaphysics does not at all imply the sense of a destruction and abolition of our tradition, but of an unbuilding, a taking apart and laying bare of the foundations upon which our thought is erected.

Derrida repeatedly paid tribute to Heidegger for his innovation in critical thought about metaphysics and emphasized that his own endeavor would not have been possible "without the opening of Heidegger's questions," and first of all, not "without the attention to what Heidegger calls the difference between Being and beings, the ontico-ontological difference such as, in a way, it remains unthought by philosophy." Because of his proximity to the Heideggerian critique of metaphysics, however, Derrida nevertheless attempted "to locate in Heidegger's text—which, no more than any other, is not homogeneous, continuous, everywhere equal to the greatest force and to all the consequences of its questions—the signs of a belonging to metaphysics, or to what he calls ontotheology." And among these "holds" of metaphysics over Heidegger, "the ultimate determination of difference as the ontico-ontological difference" appeared to Derrida "in a strange way, to be in the grasp of metaphysics."[9]

8. Martin Heidegger, *Sein und Zeit. 15th Edition with the Author's Marginal Notes* (Tübingen: Niemeyer, 1979), 19–27.

9. Jacques Derrida, "Implications," in *Positions*, trans. Alan Bass (Chicago: The University of Chicago Press, 1981), 9–10.

To expose this crucial aspect in the critique of metaphysics more fully, we should add that Heidegger developed the notion of an oblivion, a forgottenness of being in two basic forms, structural and historical. The first is carried out from the basis of phenomenology, of transcendental hermeneutics, and consists in the "analysis of existence" (*Dasein*) which marks the early work, especially *Being and Time*. This plan changed, however, and led to a turning point (*Kehre*) in Heidegger's thought because he progressively realized that phenomenology, transcendentalism, and hermeneutics themselves belong to "the history of ontology and are thus by no means capable of 'destroying' or undoing that history."[10] This is why the project of a destruction of metaphysics was carried out in terms of what Heidegger called a history of Being as metaphysics. The history of Being as metaphysics seemed to permit a position outside of history, a position without self-referentiality. Heidegger's lectures on Nietzsche are the most decisive texts on this theme.

From this point of view, the designation of Being as the truth of beings is "essentially historical" and "always demands a humankind through which it is enjoyed, grounded, communicated, and thus safeguarded" (*HN* 3:187). This is not because human history proceeds during the course of time, nor because of the actively developing and progressive character in the history of mankind, its movement in the sense of an enlightened emancipation, but because "a humankind in each case accepts the decision regarding its allotted manner of being in the midst of the truth of beings," because a humankind "is transposed (sent) into metaphysics," and because "metaphysics alone is able to ground an epoch insofar as it

10. Martin Heidegger, *The End of Philosophy*, trans. with an introduction by Joan Stambaugh (New York: Harper and Row, 1973), ix.

establishes and *maintains* a humankind in a truth concerning beings as such and as a whole" (*HN* 3:187). The historical occurrence of truth always requires from within such a humankind a particular thinker (Plato, Descartes, Leibniz, Kant, Hegel, Nietzsche) who is called upon, accepts truth's preservation, and continues the way in which "the unitary essence of metaphysics unfolds and reconstitutes itself again and again" (*HN* 3:187–88). As is obvious, it is this later theme of a history of being that links Heidegger with the postmodern end-of-philosophy discussion most directly. Derrida's image of Heidegger, however, attempts to keep the multifaceted character and always ambiguous attitude of the entire Heideggerian discourse in mind.

For the present purpose it will suffice to depict with only a few strokes the main stations in Heidegger's history of Being as metaphysics. At the beginning of Western history with Parmenides, for example, the auxiliary verb "to be" (*einai*) became a noun, "Being" (*to einai*), and thereby a concept. The most decisive step in this development occurred when Plato distinguished this Being as the ground and foundation of all beings. Plato's distinction of the Being of beings (*ontōs on, Sein des Seienden*) is precisely the ontological difference which Heidegger considers as crucial for the course of occidental metaphysics. All its implications in the sense of a prior and a later, a primary and a secondary, a ground and its surface, and also the division of being into two realms, two worlds, are already inscribed in this original distinction. Plato had determined the truth of Being as idea and specified it with the notion of *agathon,* the capable, of "what is suitable, what is good for something and itself, makes something worthwhile" (*HN* 4:169). The idea of value is implied in this conception. From now on, occidental metaphysics is idealism and Platonism, and even its earlier forms now appear as "pre-Platonic philosophy" (*N* 4:164). By determining the Being of beings as idea and ascribing to it the qualities of the good, the well-born, the high-stationed in life, Plato introduced a valorization into the ontological difference with all the implied discriminations of spirit versus matter, soul versus body, speech versus writing, and so on.

Faced with the division into Being and beings, philosophical preoccupation focused more and more on the question "*What* is Being?" in the sense of something present, objectifiable, ascertainable, manageable, and the question about Being *as* Being (*to on hē on, Sein als Sein*) became silent. The suppression of Being for the sake of something tangible went hand in hand with the self-empowering of the subject as the source of perception, the ground and master for the scientific and technological domination of Being. Descartes and Kant transformed Plato's idea to human perception and made transcendental subjectivity the condition of possibility for beings. The fateful thinking of subjectivity took hold in the West, humanizing and anthropomorphizing everything. Finally, Hegel and Nietzsche intensified the notion of human subjectivity (*animal rationale*) according to its two components—Hegel by making *rationalitas* in its speculative-dialectical form the determining principle and Nietzsche by declaring *brutalitas* and *bestialitas* the absolute essence of subjectivity (*HN* 4:148). With the progressive loss of Being, the forgottenness of Being, this process is now heading toward the end of philosophy, the end of the old world, and a total immersion in the technology and cybernetics of the "American age."

In certain instances, Heidegger depicts a distant goal for humanity in the sense of a reversal of the traditional question about the Being of beings to that of the "truth of Being" (*HN* 3:191). He himself attempted to promote this trend by taking recourse to the poetic language of Hölderlin, the thought of the pre-Socratics, or his own sibylline usage of words—all providing examples of a language that had not been perverted by the dominion of beings over Being and thereby offering some hope for a final word which would denominate Being and be wedded to Being. Yet this remained for Heidegger the "farthest goal" of history, infinitely removed from the "demonstrable events and circumstances of the present age," and belonged "to the historical remoteness of another history" (*HN* 3:191), a different age of the world. During the long interval between these ages, people will continue to think "metaphysically" and to fabricate "systems of metaphysics." Heidegger usually depicts this transitional period in gloomy terms as a time of leveling and flattening out.[11] Yet even in these dark moods, Heidegger's thought remained oriented, structurally and historically, toward a "clearing," a final word for the truth of Being as the Being *as* Being.

One can safely say that with this thinking of a Being which remains unavailable and totally unknowable, yet determines every structure of thought and poetic diction, Heidegger provided that pattern of a delayed and never fully realizable presence that is operative in post-Hegelian hermeneutics and communication theory. This is by no means the unlimited expenditure type of différance that Derrida is pursuing but still a cunning, ruseful type of restricted economy, of limited thinking—a thinking that has only stepped out of the strictures of dialectics and postponed the guaranteed final success of Hegelianism. This model of thought is operative in every "dialogical" type of thinking and understanding, in every

11. Especially in Martin Heidegger, "The End of Philosophy and the Task of Thinking," in *On Time and Being,* trans. Joan Stambaugh (New York: Harper and Row, 1972), 57–58.

form of hermeneutics and the human or social sciences that takes incompletion, failure, disruption as "structural elements of historical experience" by declaring these phenomena meaningful parts of a larger whole, links in a chain, steps toward self-fulfillment.

This model of thought, in other words, does not yet twist us out of Hegelianism. Its pattern can best be described with terms such as progressive coherence, gradual integration, genetic wholeness, enlarging of context, or ongoing continuity. This view of difference is determined by meaning and meaningfulness throughout, even if meaning is obscured in the past, does not fully occur in the present, and will not attain self-presence in the future. But the idea of a total congruity or a complete relationship of all historical phenomena is always operative in this manner of thinking. If one wanted to contrast this holistic thinking of difference, modeled after Heidegger's ontological difference, with Derrida's différance, one would have to use phrases like "discontinuous restructuring" for the latter and employ a model of thought that is based neither on a prospective nor a retrospective foundation of truth, that readily admits lack of coherence and congruity, radical unpredictability, and incomprehensibility, however, not as deficiencies but as the factual form of our knowledge.[12]

3

Yet, as his recurring impact upon our time manifests, Heidegger cannot be categorized and dismissed that easily. Through special strategies of double gesticulation, his

12. See on this Ernst Behler, "Deconstruction versus Hermeneutics: Derrida and Gadamer on Text and Interpretation," in *Southern Humanities Review* 21 (1983): 201–23.

thought escapes unilateral definition and is often a step ahead of the interpreter. As far as meaning and lack of meaning within the structure of ontological difference and the ensuing history of Being as metaphysics is concerned, Heidegger's later writings present some baffling versions. They usually occur when he attempts to think "in Greek fashion" and gives familiar concepts an interesting new twist. Forgottenness is such an instance because, thought of in the Greek way, it has not only the active meaning of having forgotten ("I have forgotten my umbrella") but also the passive one of an occurrence, a fate. Forgottenness of Being in this subtle sense is a destiny occurring to us because Being has withdrawn and is concealing itself.[13] Although the concealment of Being is still based on the model of presence and clearing, it describes the absence of Being not as a result of human failure and historical condition, but as a structural relationship of absence.

Concealment can also be thought of "in Greek fashion" and it then manifests a disarming double gesture of concealing and revealing. Limit (*peras*) is another paradigm of Greek thinking, if one emphasizes not only that where something ends, but simultaneously, that in which something originates, in which something stands and is shaped in its particular form and made present as the same.[14] With such modes of thinking, Heidegger anticipates Derrida's conception of phenomena such as "trace," that is, genuine forms of différance. Such models of thought also remind us of the fact that deconstructive thinking is not a mere negation of meaning and system but that fine line of thinking in between presence and absence,

13. Martin Heidegger, "Zur Seinsfrage," in *Martin Heidegger, Wegmarken* (Frankfurt: Klostermann, 1967), 243.

14. Martin Heidegger, *Parmenides,* ed. Manfred S. Frings (Frankfurt: Klostermann, 1982).

system and nonsystem, order and chaos, revealing and concealing. In this sense, Friedrich Schlegel said: "It is equally fatal for the mind to have a system, and to have none. One will simply have to decide to combine the two" (*FS* 2:173).

A similar double aspect is conveyed by Heidegger's notion of Western metaphysics as progressive nihilism and his conception of the "utterly completed, perfect nihilism as the fulfillment of nihilism proper" (*HN* 4:203). At first glance, nihilism indicates failure, omission, lack, and defeat. By construing the highest possibility and the total perfection of metaphysics as an absolute manifestation of nihilism, however, and as the complete devaluation of all values so far declared as values, Heidegger's thought assumes its characteristic shape. At the beginning of occidental metaphysics stands Plato's declaration of the highest form of Being as heavenly ideas, at the end the revelation of Being as vital forces here on earth, as will to power, involved in a senseless reoccurrence of the same. That is the inner law of metaphysical thinking, its irreversible course. Nihilism, properly speaking, is therefore much more than the outcome, the result, the end of the history of metaphysics. Nihilism is not merely a "doctrine or an opinion," not the simple "dissolution of everything into mere nothingness," but the process of devaluating those highest values which in the history of metaphysics were declared, one after the other, as the truth of Being and then lost their capacity to shape history (*HN* 3:203).

This process is not one "historical occurrence among many others," but rather "the fundamental event of occidental history, which has been sustained and guided by metaphysics" and drives in its last act to a complete "revaluation of previous values" (*HN* 3:203). Nihilism is the "lawfulness of this historic occurrence, its 'logic'" (*HN* 3:205). Nihilism for Heidegger does not propel us into mere nothingness, but its "true essence lies in its affirmative manner of liberation" (*HN* 3:204). "Perfection of nihilism" is lastly nothing but another name for perfection of metaphysics, in that nihilism and metaphysics are congruent for Heidegger. Nihilism is the most decisive aspect in the history of Being as metaphysics.[15] Because of this interrelationship, Heidegger, as perhaps no one before him, was able to think of the previous history of Western metaphysics as a unified whole. One will have to add, however, that the figures in Heidegger's history of Being as metaphysics are little more than colorless abstracts and that the thoughts of the great philosophers are reduced not only to history, but worse, to a scheme.

Derrida is fully aware of this ambiguity in Heidegger and attempts to protect and maintain it more than any other of Heidegger's contemporary readers. Already in *Of Grammatology* he saw Heidegger's philosophy at once contained in and transgressing the metaphysics of presence. "The very moment of transgression sometimes holds it back short of the limit," he said (*OG*, 22).[16] By limiting the sense of Being to presence, Heidegger remained within the dominion of Western metaphysics for Derrida; by questioning the origin of that domination, however, Heidegger came to a questioning of what constitutes our history. Heidegger brings this up when in his writing *On the Question of Being,* he has the word Being crossed out in his text: *Sein*.[17] "That mark of deletion," Derrida says, "is not, however, a 'merely negative symbol.' That deletion is the final writing of an epoch. Under its strokes the presence of a transcendental signified is effaced while still remaining

15. Especially in Heidegger, *Nietzsche,* vol. 4, *European Nihilism.*

16. Jacques Derrida, *Of Grammatology,* trans. Gayatri Chakravorty Spivak (Baltimore: The Johns Hopkins University Press, 1974). References to this text are designated *OG.*

17. See Heidegger, "Zur Seinsfrage."

legible" (*OG*, 23). Such hesitation of thought is not "incoherence," Derrida continues, but a "trembling proper to all post-Hegelian attempts and to this passage between two epochs" (*OG*, 24).

This is why in *Différance* Derrida sees no "simple answer" to the question of whether Heidegger's thought is still an "intrametaphysical effect of différance" or the "deployment of différance" (*D*, 153). We could say that Heidegger's ontological difference between Being and beings and the disappearance of the truth of Being is only a partial aspect of différance, that différance is a more comprehensive, more all-pervasive model of thought than ontological difference, or to use the historical way of putting it, that différance is "'older' than the ontological difference or the truth of Being" (*D*, 154). Yet nobody knew better about the "epochality" of his history of Being as metaphysics than Heidegger, and Derrida himself insists that "we must stay within the difficulty of this passage" and "repeat this passage in a rigorous reading of metaphysics wherever metaphysics serves as the norm of Western speech, and not only in the texts of 'the history of Western philosophy'" (*D*, 154).

A more basic point concerning Heidegger is brought up by Derrida with the question: "How do we conceive of the outside of a text?" (*D*, 158). This does not refer only to the epochality of occidental metaphysics and to the problem of how "we conceive of what stands opposed to the text of Western metaphysics" (*D*, 158). This question relates to the much more fundamental attempt at going "beyond the history of Being, beyond our language as well, and beyond everything that can be named by it" (*D*, 157). This attempt was the motivating force of metaphysics and its successive efforts to denominate the truth of Being, and to ground the structurality of structure in a principle outside of it, or to transcend the rules of the game. Heidegger had been the most eloquent critic of these metaphysical attempts but still conceived of an outside of the text through his nostalgia and hope for the "marriage between speech and Being in the unique word, in the finally proper name" (*D,* 160). For Derrida, however, consequently, there is no "outside of a text" ("*il n'y a pas de hors text*" [*OG,* 158]), and there "will be no unique name, not even the name of Being." Yet this situation must be taken "without nostalgia," Derrida insists: "that is, it must be conceived outside the myth of the purely maternal or paternal language belonging to the lost fatherland of thought. On the contrary, we must *affirm* it—in the sense that Nietzsche brings affirmation into play—with a certain laughter and a certain dance" (*D,* 159).

Formulating the same thought in contrast to the structuralist mode of thinking, Derrida distinguishes between the "saddened, *negative,* nostalgic, guilty, Rousseauistic side of the thinking of play," that of "broken immediacy," and the "Nietzschean *affirmation*" of play, that is, "the joyous affirmation of the play of the world and of the innocence of becoming, the affirmation of a world of signs without fault, without truth, and without origin which is offered an active interpretation" (*SSP,* 292).[18] The activity of this affirmation and interpretation consists precisely in determining "the noncenter otherwise than as loss of center." In its security about play and self-assuredness about playing, this affirmation "also surrenders itself to *genetic* indetermination, to the *seminal* adventure of the trace" (*SSP,* 292)—an adventure that is proclaiming itself "under the species of the nonspecies, in the formless, mute, infant, and terrifying form of monstrosity" (*SSP,* 293).

18. Jacques Derrida, "Structure, Sign, and Play in the Discourse of the Human Sciences," in *Writing and Difference,* trans. Alan Bass (Chicago: The University of Chicago Press, 1978). References to this text are designated *SSP.*

4

Yet in spite of all this self-conscious reflectiveness and self-referential awareness in the subversion of inherited structures, the most fundamental charge against this discourse in contemporary thought is that of an implied self-contradiction in criticizing truth and philosophy: "The totalizing self-critique of reason gets caught in a performative contradiction, since subject-centered reason can be convicted of being authoritarian in nature only by having recourse to its own tools" (*DM*, 185).[19] This is a quote from Habermas, one of the main critics of the deconstruction of reason and metaphysics. It is most directly pronounced against Adorno's critique of the Enlightenment, but equally addressed to Schlegel, Nietzsche, and Derrida. Indeed, Habermas sees a direct line of development in the destruction of reason from Schlegel to Nietzsche and Derrida. Adorno and Heidegger occupy special positions on this way. Adorno resolutely "practices determinate negation unremittingly, even though it has lost any foothold in the categorical network of Hegelian logic" (*DM*, 186). Heidegger, in contrast, "flees from this paradox to the luminous heights of an esoteric, special discourse, which absolves itself of the restrictions of discursive speech generally and is immunized by vagueness against any specific objections" (*DM*, 185). All the other critiques of deconstructive thought and ironic discourse—relapse into myth and religion, escape into literature and poetry, political disinterest, social aloofness, lack of practice—follow from this basic critique.

19. Jürgen Habermas, *The Philosophical Discourse of Modernity*, trans. Frederick Lawrence (Cambridge: MIT Press, 1987). References to this text are designated *DM*. For a critique of Habermas's presentation of Nietzsche as a return to the archaic and a relapse into myth, see David E. Wellbery, "Nietzsche-Art-Postmodernism: A Reply to Jürgen Habermas," *Stanford Italian Review* (1986), 77–100.

Nietzsche is considered the "turntable" for this development according to Habermas, since he is the first in history to renounce a renewed revision of the concept of reason and "*bids farewell* to the dialectic of enlightenment" (*DM,* 86). He rejected the very "achievements of modernity," that "from which the modern age drew its pride and self-consciousness," that is, subjective freedom realized in society (*DM,* 83), in order "to gain a foothold in myth as the other of reason" (*DM,* 86). With Nietzsche, "modernity loses its single status" and merely constitutes "a last epoch in the far-reaching history of a rationalization initiated by the dissolution of archaic life and the collapse of myth" (*DM,* 87). A utopian attitude now focuses on the "god who *is coming,*" and a "religious festival become work of art" is supposed to bridge the modern age with the archaic (*DM,* 87).

For Habermas, however, Nietzsche was by no means original in his "Dionysian treatment of history" (*DM,* 92). His thesis about the origin of the tragic chorus in the rites of Dionysus derives "from a context that was already well developed in early romanticism" (*DM,* 92), and the idea of a new mythology is just as much of "romantic provenance" as the "recourse to Dionysus as the god who is coming" (*DM,* 88). Habermas finds the expectation of a new mythology to replace philosophy in Schelling and in other texts from the turn of the eighteenth century, but especially in Friedrich Schlegel (*DM,* 88–89). Schlegel indeed published a *Speech on Mythology* in 1800 demanding the creation of a "focal point, such as mythology was for the ancients" (*FS* 2:312). Habermas understands this demand as postulating an absolute position of poetry above reason, a "becoming aesthetic of ideas that are supposed to be joined in this way with the interests of the people" (*DM,* 90), a surrendering to the "world of the primordial forces of myth" (*DM,* 90–91), a return into the "primordial chaos of human nature" (*DM*, 90; *KFSA* 2:319), a "messianic temporalizing of what for Schelling was a well-founded historical expectation" (*DM*, 90), and altogether an increased valuation of "Dionysus, the driven god of frenzy, of madness, and of ceaseless transformations" (*DM*, 91). To leave no doubt as to the position from which he argues, Habermas adds polemically: "The difference from Hegel is obvious—not speculative reason, but poetry alone can, as soon as it becomes public in the form of a new mythology, replace the unifying power of religion" (*DM*, 89).

Whereas the romantic recourse to Dionysus served as a byway to the fulfillment of Christian promises annulled by the Reformation and the Enlightenment (*DM*, 92), Habermas claims, Nietzsche cleansed the Dionysian of such romantic elements and enhanced it to the absolute self-oblivion of subjectivity in a blissful ecstasy. Only when all "categories of intelligent doing and thinking are upset, the norms of daily life have broken down," and "the illusions of habitual normality have collapsed" (*DM*, 93), can the modern human being expect from the new mythology "a kind of redemption that eliminates all mediations" (*DM*, 94). Only then do we reach "reason's absolute other," that is, experiences that are displaced back into the archaic realm—"experiences of self-disclosure of a decentered subjectivity, liberated from all constraints of cognition and purposive activity, all imperatives of utility and morality" (*DM*, 94).

From now on, however, the Nietzsche of Habermas begins to resemble more and more a specter. Without any concern for textual evidence, Habermas depicts him as a pragmatic epistemologist who denied any difference between true and false, good and evil, and reduced such distinctions to "preferences for what serves life and for the noble" (*DM*, 95). The "transsubjective will to power is manifested in the ebb and flow of an anonymous process of subjugation" (*DM*, 95), and the dominion of "subject-centered reason" in the modern age is seen as "the result and expression of a perversion of the will to power" (*DM*, 95), as nihilism. Nietzsche attempted to give meaning to the nihilism of his time by supposedly declaring it as "the night of the remoteness of the gods, in which the proximity of the absent god is proclaimed." Yet he could not "legitimize" the criteria of his aesthetic judgments because he had transposed them into the archaic and did not recognize them as a "moment of reason" (*DM*, 96).

These disclosures of power theories undertaken for the sake of the aesthetic, the "gateway to the Dionysian," constitute for Habermas Nietzsche's particular "dilemma of a self-enclosed critique of reason that has become total" (*DM*, 96). Habermas believes that Nietzsche could muster "no clarity about what it means to pursue a critique of ideology that attacks its own foundations" (*DM*, 96), a "totalized, self-consuming critique of ideology" (*DM*, 97). The two poles, reason and its other, do not stand in a dialectical relationship to each other, mutually negating and thereby enhancing each other, but in a relationship of "mutual repugnance and exclusion." Reason is "delivered over to the dynamics of withdrawal and retreat, of expulsion and proscription," whereas "self-reflection is sealed off from the other of reason" (*DM*, 103). Habermas's final verdict on Nietzsche is: "His theory of power cannot satisfy the claim to scientific objectivity and, at the same time, put into effect the program of a total and hence self-referential critique of reason that also affects the truth of theoretical propositions" (*DM*, 104–5).

Whereas the self-referential contradiction in the case of Nietzsche is derived from an assumed theory of power for the sake of a Dionysian aestheticism, Derrida's self-contradiction is construed from an alleged, yet futile search for an arche-writing on the part of the French philosopher—an arche-writing which has been lost and of which we find only traces in a strange, obliterated, Kafkaesque shape (*DM*, 164). The increasing degree of subject-centered reason, of the categorical network of Hegelian logic, of a dialectic of enlightenment, and of modernity from Schlegel to Nietzsche and Derrida is obviously accompanied for Habermas by an increase in self-contradiction which, with Derrida, now comes to a new height. Yet the special trait in Habermas's image of Derrida derives from his assertion that the latter's "program of a scripture scholarship with claims to a critique of metaphysics" has an alleged religious inspiration, is "nourished from religious sources" (*DM*, 165). Derrida's thought of an "arche-writing prior to all identifiable inscriptions" (*DM*, 179) is seen by Habermas as the "remembrance of the messianism of Jewish mysticism and of the abandoned but well-circumscribed place once assumed by the God of the Old Testament" (*DM*, 167), more precisely, the Torah in its inexhaustibility (*DM*, 182) and the "mystical concept of tradition as an ever *delayed* event of revelation" (*DM*, 183).

This notion of an arche-writing drives Derrida back behind Heidegger (*DM*, 183), according to Habermas. He characterizes Derrida's attempt as "going beyond the ontological difference and Being to the difference proper to writing, which puts an origin already set in motion [Heidegger's Being] yet one level deeper" (*DM*, 181). Arche-writing, in other words, "takes on the role of a subjectless generator of structures," of structures without an author (*DM*, 180). Yet Habermas regards Derrida's distinction from Heidegger as "insignificant" (*DM*, 181) because Derrida "does not shake loose of the intentions of a first philosophy" and "lands at an empty, formula-like avowal of some indeterminate authority." The only difference between the two philosophers is that in Derrida's case this is "not the authority of a Being that has been distorted by beings, but the authority of a no longer holy scripture, of a scripture that is in exile, wandering about, estranged from its own meaning, a scripture that testamentarily documents the absence of the holy" (*DM,* 181).

The other main objection Habermas raises against Derrida also relates to the alleged self-referential contradiction and concerns the "leveling of genre distinction between literature and philosophy" in deconstructive theory (*DM,* 185). Derrida and his followers abolished the borderlines between philosophy and literature, as Habermas sees it, in order to escape the "consistency requirements" of scientific discourse. Derrida thereby "*undercuts*" the problem of self-referentiality and makes it irrelevant; he simply attempts to "*clear away* the ontological *scaffolding* erected by philosophy in the course of its subject-centered history of reason" (*DM,* 188–89). Yet he does this not "analytically, in the sense of identifying hidden presuppositions or implications," as one usually does, but "by a critique of style, in that he finds something like indirect communications, by which the text itself denies its manifest content, in the rhetorical surplus of meaning inherent in the literary strata of texts that present themselves as non-literary" (*DM,* 189).

What is bothering Habermas, however, is that Derrida applies this reading technique not only to texts by Kafka, Joyce, and Celan, but also to those of Husserl, Saussure, and Rousseau, and interprets them "against the explicit interpretations of their authors" (*DM,* 189). The goal of this strategy appears to be obvious to Habermas: "As soon as we take the *literary* character of Nietzsche's writings seriously, the suitableness of his critique of reason has to be assessed in accord with the standards of rhetorical success and not those of logical consistency" (*DM,* 188). Yet Habermas is of the opinion that such a procedure is legitimate only "if the philosophical text is *in truth* a literary one—if one can *demonstrate* that the genre distinction between philosophy and literature dissolves upon closer examination" (*DM,* 189). The positive result of such an examination would apparently constitute a dangerous and frightening situation for Habermas because it would lead to an upgrading of literary criticism to a critique of metaphysics and would grant literary criticism, *horribile dictu,* the status of a "procedure that takes on an almost world-historical mission with its overcoming of the thinking of the metaphysics of presence and of the age of logocentrism" (*DM,* 191–92). To avoid such mingling of departments and academic disciplines, Habermas devotes the rest of his Derrida critique to an elaboration of the distinctiveness and exclusiveness of poetic speech.

To reduce the discussion partner's importance and eventually exclude him from the solution of the problem, thereby silencing him, is the most typical gesture for this type of consensus-finding through communication, especially if the other side stands in opposition to or is not easily accommodated by the intended purpose. This attitude can already be noticed in Habermas's treatment of Friedrich Schlegel who, because of his *Speech on Mythology,* is put down as an irrationalist of the poetic sort. In reality, however, the *Speech on Mythology* is part of a larger text, the *Dialogue on Poetry,* depicting a group of animated and witty conversational partners who discuss possibilities of how "to bring poetry the closest to the highest possible poetry at all on earth" (*FS* 2:286). Four formal presentations are made outlining different approaches to this goal, one of which is the *Speech on Mythology.*

We can assume with good reason that the entire text attempts to convey an image of the Jena group of early German romanticism and that each conversational partner enacts a certain role in this scene. If this assumption is correct or even acceptable, however, the speaker for the new mythology is probably the philosopher Schelling because of Schelling's own historical preoccupation with the theme and because of a certain rashness and impetuosity in his style ("I will go right to the point. . . ." [*FS* 2:312]). In this case the *Speech on Mythology* would not only constitute a programmatic, apodictic statement on the necessity of a new mythology and the desire to create one, but would also incorporate Schlegel's critical assessment of such a project in a highly conscious though entirely indirect manner of communication.

In the last analysis, however, the *Speech on Mythology* remains Schlegel's own text in spite of all this framing, distancing, and configuring, and it matters little whether Schlegel attributed the postulate of a new mythology to Schelling, himself, or to an entirely fictitious figure named Lothario. What matters, however, is the structuring of the text, namely, the integration of a highly self-critical and self-conscious attitude about mythology with a writing on mythology, that is, irony, self-creation and self-destruction. Yet all these sophisticated modes of communication are ignored in Habermas's reading of the *Speech on Mythology*, and the text is reduced to a straightforward statement by Schlegel. Not even its character as speech, as a rhetorical expression indicated in the title, is noticed. Hegel called Schlegel by all sorts of names and considered him to be insolent, vain, destructive, and not really interested in the real concerns of humanity. Yet Hegel would never have characterized Schlegel as unreflective, as conceiving of poetry as "cleansed of associations with theoretical and practical reason," as opening "the door to the world of the primordial forces of myth" (*DM*, 90–91). Even a restricted reading of the *Speech on Mythology* outside of any context should come to the discovery that Schlegel did not conceive of the new mythology in terms of a relapse into myth but as something "forged from the deepest depth of the mind," as the "most artful of all works of art" (*FS* 2:312).

The neglect of style and of the "literary" mode of communication must lead to disastrous results in Habermas's critique of Nietzsche, for whom the structuring of a text, the seriousness of the *mise en scène,* was a primary requirement for intellectuality, for writing. Habermas's reading of Nietzsche indeed leads to the assumption of a ruthless Renaissance aestheticism in the style of "Nothing is true, everything is permitted." The active interdependence among all of Nietzsche's statements is totally ignored. Nietzsche is reduced to someone who had "no clarity about what it means to pursue a critique of ideology that attacks its own foundations" (*DM,* 96)—as if an ideology critique that does *not* attack its own foundations were necessarily superior. The problem with this kind of argumentation is that whoever does not conform to a certain trend of philosophizing, here a revised Hegelianism, is excluded from philosophical discourse and declared a romantic, a protofascist, a Jewish mystic, or an American literary critic. A radicalized or "totalized" critique of reason appears to be prohibited because of the offense by such a critique against basic rules and conventions of "philosophical" argumentation. So coercion-free communication begins with coercion to accept these norms.

5

Rorty sees no problem with a totalized critique of reason and philosophy and would at the most question its usefulness. He also has no objection to breaking down the borderlines between philosophy and literature and considers such departmentalizations simply habits, which, however, often carry along wrong hierarchical concepts of knowledge. For him, the invention of romantic poetry was an event just as important in the modern world as any comparable innovation in the realm of the sciences and philosophy. Of the two types of philosophy, Kant and Hegel, Habermas and Lyotard, truth-oriented and interpretation-oriented thinking, decentering and disseminative thought, which he likes to play off against each other, Rorty seems to favor the latter because of its higher level of reflection and self-criticism. "The first likes to present itself as a straightforward, down-to-earth, scientific attempt to get things right," he says:

> The second needs to present itself obliquely, with the help of as many foreign words and as much allusiveness and name-dropping as possible. Neo-Kantian philosophers like Putnam, Strawson, and Rawls have arguments and theses which are connected to Kant's by a fairly straightforward series of "purifying" transformations, transformations which are thought to give clearer and clearer views of the persistent problems. For the non-Kantian philosophers, there are no persistent problems—save perhaps the existence of Kantians. Non-Kantian philosophers like Heidegger and Derrida are emblematic figures who not only do not solve problems, they do not *have* arguments and theses. They are connected with their predecessors not by common subjects or methods but in the "family resemblance" way in which latecomers in a sequence of commentators on commentators are connected with older members of the same sequence.[20]

In a recent book, Rorty presents these two types of philosophers with the names of "metaphysicians" and "ironists."[21]

20. Richard Rorty, "Philosophy as a Kind of Writing: An Essay on Derrida," in *Consequences of Pragmatism* (Minneapolis: University of Minnesota Press, 1982), 92–93.

21. Richard Rorty, *Contingency, Irony, and Solidarity* (Cambridge: Cambridge University Press, 1989). References to this text are designated *CIS*.

The tradition of "ironist philosophy" began with the early Hegel and continued with Nietzsche, Heidegger, and Derrida (*CIS*, 78), whereas metaphysical philosophy is an attempt at "grounding" one's beliefs and presenting them as proven, as truth. Such a ground can be as shaky as Habermas's communication theory and still qualify the proponent as a metaphysician (*CIS*, 82). It is the intention that counts. Ironists, in contrast, do not believe in grounds. They rename and redefine problems instead and engage in endless metonymies.

Rorty's canon of ironist philosophy is almost identical to the one in our text. Instead of Friedrich Schlegel, he includes the early Hegel of the *Phenomenology of Spirit*, but the real difference is Heidegger, who in the present study appears as an ironist only in certain borderline cases such as his thinking "in Greek fashion." This difference is of importance for the understanding of irony and should therefore be explained right away. Rorty knows of course that Heidegger "spent a lot of time being scornful of the aestheticist, pragmatist, lightmindedness of the ironist": "He thought of them as dilettantish clatterers who lacked the high seriousness of the great metaphysicians—their special relation to Being. As a Schwarzwald redneck, he had an ingrained dislike of the North German cosmopolitan mandarins. As a philosopher, he viewed the rise of the ironist intellectuals—many of them Jews—as symptomatic of the degeneracy of what he called 'the age of the world picture'" (*CIS*, 111–12).

Looked at from the perspective of the history of Being as metaphysics, the age of irony would have begun for Heidegger with the demise of metaphysics in the Occident, with the closure of the "epoch," around the end of the Second World War, although he never described this development in terms of irony. This is a period of a general flattening out, of disbelief, of the degeneration of philosophy into anthropology and psychology, of its transformation into the individual sciences, of cybernetics and the computer. It is a period of a completely indeterminable length before a new age of the world can begin.[22] We could also call it the postmodern age, because many postmodern features correspond precisely to Heidegger's descriptions of the state of affairs after all "*essential possibilities* of metaphysics are exhausted" in the Occident (*N* 4:148). Yet Heidegger never wanted simply to brush off metaphysics as the ironist does in Rorty's description, but maintained a most solemn memory (*Andenken*) of it and still attempted to say the ultimate word by uttering Hölderlin's verses or the fragments by the pre-Socratics. This solemn, hymnical, spellbound attitude appears to be the opposite of irony and seems to exclude Heidegger from the ironic discourse of modernity.

The reason that Rorty includes Heidegger among the great ironists of our time is not so much his occasional twisting of words and concepts, which thereby assume a self-referential deprecation of his own position, but rather a special notion of irony or of ironist theory based on the idea "that something (history, Western man, metaphysics—something large enough to have a destiny) has exhausted its possibilities" (*CIS*, 101). For Rorty, the ironist assumes the role of "the last philosopher" (*CIS*, 106) and treats all the former ones as metaphysicians (*CIS*, 110). The ironist knows that there is no truth and that the role of philosophy now has to be played entirely differently.

The special point in Rorty's new discussion of metaphysicians and ironists is, however, that he puts the two to the test of pragmatism and asks what they are worth in terms of social

22. Martin Heidegger, *The End of Philosophy*, trans. with an introduction by Joan Stambaugh (New York: Harper and Row, 1973).

engineering, liberal politics, and human solidarity. His test turns out to be bad for both, but worse for the ironist. Habermas, for instance, sees the function of metaphysical philosophy as supplying "some social glue which will replace religious belief" and finds it in the "universality" of human rationality (*CIS*, 83). This is a good intention, but is based on the "ludicrous" assumption for Rorty that liberal societies are bound together by philosophical beliefs (*CIS*, 86). "Absence of metaphysics" is by no means politically dangerous, as one might assume, no more than atheism weakened "liberal societies" as people feared in the nineteenth century. On the contrary, it "strengthened them" (*CIS*, 85). Rorty easily dismisses Habermas's fear that "ironist thinking which runs from Hegel through Foucault and Derrida" is destructive of social hope. He rather sees "this line of thought as largely irrelevant to public life and to political questions," making the point: "Ironist theorists like Hegel, Nietzsche, Derrida and Foucault seem to me to be invaluable in our attempt to form a private self-image, but pretty well useless when it comes to politics" (*CIS*, 83).

In pursuing this point more closely, Rorty asks questions such as whether ironism is "compatible with a sense of human solidarity" (*CIS*, 87), with a "universalistic ethics" (*CIS*, 88), or with hope (*CIS*, 91) and always comes to a negative result combined with the feeling that "there is something right about the suspicion which ironism arouses" (*CIS*, 89). One would readily admit in the intellectual climate of today, he argues, that public rhetoric in a "liberal culture" should be "nominalist and historicist," that is, nonmetaphysical, and one should consider this "both possible and desirable." Yet one would hardly go on "to claim that there could be or ought to be a culture whose public rhetoric is *ironist*" (*CIS*, 87). Rorty's ideal candidate for public rhetoric in a liberal culture would be a "common-sensically nominalist and historicist" language (*CIS,* 87) that would produce "a kind of straightforward, un-self-conscious, transparent prose—precisely the kind of prose no self-creating ironist wants to write" (*CIS,* 89). Philosophy, in the increasingly self-conscious culture of today, "has become more important for the pursuit of private perfection rather than of any social task" (*CIS,* 94) and should therefore not be asked "to do a job which it cannot do, and which it defines itself as unable to do" (*CIS,* 94).

Another good candidate for promoting human solidarity and the liberal cause of hope and political utility is poetry and literature, especially the novel (*CIS,* 94, 96). Ethnographic descriptions and other "non-theoretical literary genres" are also suited for this task because of their direct impact. We thereby come to a strong division, a "split," as Rorty says, between the private and the public sector, theory and practice, literature and philosophy. Philosophy, especially in its contemporary sophisticated status of theory and irony, is assigned to the private realm, whereas the public domain is handed over to common sense and literature. In former times, while still pursuing the project of modernity during the period of philosophy as metaphysics, one had hoped "to bring together our private and our public lives by showing us that self-discovery and political utility could be united" (*CIS,* 120). Now we should "stop trying to combine self-creation and politics, especially if we are liberals" because the political part of a liberal ironist's final vocabulary "will never integrate with the rest of that vocabulary" (*CIS,* 120).

6

The epitome of irony in this end-of-philosophy style is for Rorty, consequently, one kind of writing practiced by Derrida. Rorty does not, however, refer so much to the poststructuralist and post-Heideggerian Derrida whom we have discussed in previous sections. For in these early texts there is still too much talk of "infrastructures," of "undercutting," of "conditions of possibility," of "presence as absence," in other words, of very metaphysical sounding notions. These texts at least lend themselves to such readings and inspire research projects on grammatology or epochal distinctions in the sense of "the end of the book and the beginning of writing." Rorty turns to later writings such as *The Truth in Painting* (1978), *Glas* (1981), but especially *The Postcard* (1980), and to the section "Envois" of the latter,[23] in which interconnective thought processes are abandoned for the sake of freely spinning fantasies. According to Rorty, Derrida now gives "free rein to the trains of associations," and such daydreaming is in Rorty's view "the end product of ironist theorizing" (*CIS*, 125).

Derrida's alleged retreat into "private fantasy" is for Rorty also "the only solution to the self-referential problem which such theorizing encounters, the problem of how to distance one's predecessors without doing exactly what one has repudiated them for doing" (*CIS*, 125). Rorty says: "So I take Derrida's importance to lie in having had the courage to give up the attempt to unite the private and the public, to stop trying to bring together a quest for private autonomy, and an attempt at public resonance and utility. He privatizes the sublime, having learned from the fate of his predecessors that the public can never be more than beautiful" (*CIS*, 125). Derrida thereby brings to conclusion a philosophical trend beginning with Hegel which had been haunted by ever deeper layers of foundation in its deconstructive drive. At

23. Jacques Derrida, *The Postcard*, trans. Alan Bass (Chicago: The University of Chicago Press, 1987), 1–257.

least, this philosophical movement had been interpreted from outside as forever coming up with always new and profounder grounds for being: Hegel with reason, Nietzsche with the will to power, Heidegger with Being, and Derrida with an arche-writing. Rorty comments:

> I am claiming that Derrida, in "Envois," has written a kind of book which nobody had ever thought of before. He has done for the history of philosophy what Proust did for his own life story: He has played all the authority figures, and all the descriptions of himself which these figures might be imagined as giving, off against each other, with the result that the very notion of "authority" loses application in reference to his work. He has achieved autonomy in the same way that Proust achieved autonomy: neither *Remembrance of Things Past* nor "Envois" fits within any conceptual scheme previously used to evaluate novels or philosophical treatises. He has avoided Heideggerian nostalgia in the same way that Proust avoided sentimental nostalgia—by incessantly recontextualizing whatever memory brings back. Both he and Proust have extended the bounds of possibility. *(CIS,* 137)

We could just as well say that in this view Derrida has transgressed the realm of irony circumscribed earlier as walking the fine line inbetween system and nonsystem, chaos and order, self-creation and self-destruction—never succumbing to the one or to the other. Rorty offers us clear-cut divisions between the private and the public, reserving sophisticated theory for the personal and thumb-rule decisions for the social realm, and eliminating irony not only from the political but also from the individual sphere if the latter is seen in accomplished isolation. For what makes Hegel, Heidegger, and Derrida ironic, beyond Rorty's concept of "ironism" in the end-of-philosophy sense, is precisely that they never disentangle themselves from the entwining of metaphysics, that they never land in a value-free beyond, that they never hit rock-bottom but remain in the zone of the inbetween. Rorty's notions of a full arrival or a complete separation, his thinking in ideal types of the truly practical and the genuinely theoretical appear to be "terribly metaphysical" and extremely close to Habermas only with inverted evaluations. Derrida appears like someone who threw away the ladder of deconstruction after he had arrived in the promised land of free-spinning writing without a trace of interconnectedness among his thoughts. Ironic writing has this trend as one essential element, that of self-destruction, but never constitutes itself without the opposite, self-creation. The interrelationship between the two is so intense that we do not know which is the destructive and which is the constructive part. This writing with two hands is not only exercised in one and the same text but also proceeds alternately and alternatively. Consequently, and with the rigor of a writing that is, in Schlegel's words, entirely involuntary and yet completely deliberate, perfectly instinctive and perfectly conscious, Derrida takes up the problem of responsibility in one of his very "latest" texts, even that of political responsibility.[24]

In this context, but also in others and especially in that of postmodernism, it appears highly significant that the three star-witnesses for the discourse of modernity and irony as the main structural principle of that discourse, Schlegel, Nietzsche, and Derrida, do not see irony in a developmental scheme as the last accomplishment of a late epoch, but assign it a much more fundamental function. One could even doubt, with good reason, that Schlegel, Nietzsche, and Derrida actually believed in the origin of a modern period distinguishing us from the rest of the world. In the quote about the rupture

24. Jacques Derrida, "Like the Sound of the Sea Deep within a Shell: Paul de Man's War," *Critical Inquiry* 14 (1988): 590–625.

or disrupture which marked our epoch, Derrida added that this rupture had "always already begun to proclaim itself and begun to work" (*SSP*, 280). Nietzsche used the term "modern" almost exclusively in deprecatory manner. And Schlegel, when pressed to give a date for the beginning of the modern age, first mentioned Euripides, soon added Socrates, and then shifted to Pythagoras because he was for him the one who for the first time thought about the entirety of the whole world from the principle of one single idea. What these examples suggest is that for Schlegel, Nietzsche, and Derrida a radical type of reflective thinking was not the prerogative of an epoch but an eternal mark of man. If they had to date the postmodern period, and they are great authorities in matters of irony and the postmodern, they would have given an amazingly early date and let it coincide with the origin of man or, if there is no such origin, with the eternal transgression of man.

This does not exclude a sense for history. However, if we had to locate the ironies of Schlegel, Nietzsche, and Derrida in any historical context, we would have to choose classical Greece and, strangely enough, Plato's Academy. This appears to be strange because Nietzsche and Derrida, not Schlegel, are highly critical of Plato: Nietzsche by proclaiming Plato as the originator of the metaphysics of two worlds, which implied a defamation of our world and made Christianity "Platonism for the people" (*FN* 5:12); and Derrida by considering Plato the father of logocentrism and phonocentrism with all the implied binary discriminations of spirit versus matter, soul versus body, speech versus writing, man versus woman.

And yet, all three saw Plato also as the prototype of a philosopher whom, had they believed in a postmodern era, they could have very well prescribed for that time as a model. In a text that became the source for one of the most influential

Plato receptions in modern history, Schlegel wrote: "Plato, although he very well had a philosophy, had yet no system, just as philosophy itself is altogether more a search, a striving for science than science itself. And this is especially the case with that of Plato. He never completed his thought. This continuously endeavoring movement of his mind for perfected knowledge and understanding of the highest, this constant becoming, shaping, and developing of his ideas, he attempted to write down artistically in dialogues" (*FS* 11:120). Nietzsche considered it the most revealing feature about Plato that a copy of Aristophanes was discovered under the pillow of his deathbed. "How could he have endured life," Nietzsche exclaimed, "Greek life, to which he said no, without Aristophanes!" (*FN* 5:47; *GE*, 41). And in Derrida's reading of Plato as the king of logocentrism with his sun-filled voice who condemned the arts, play, rhetoric, writing, and myth, the Greek philosopher does all this in a text, the very essence of which consists of art, play, rhetoric, performative writing, and mythical accounts. Plato's text can justly be considered the prototype for Derrida's own predilection for the dissimulation of the woven texture; it is indeed the text *par excellence* for him, and also a text which has been misread for millennia and has always new discoveries in store once we open it.[25] When Heidegger declared Plato the originator of occidental metaphysics, he made the Greek philosopher, to a certain degree, the inaugurator of the modern age. Derrida, in his deconstructive reading, shows the contradictory overabundance in Plato and thereby makes him the initiator of the postmodern epoch—if there were such a thing.

25. Jacques Derrida, "Plato's Pharmacy," in *Dissemination*, trans. Barbara Johnson (Chicago: The University of Chicago Press, 1981), 61–171.

Index of Names